Challenges and Choices for Crime-Fighting Technology

Federal Support of State and Local Law Enforcement

William Schwabe • Lois M. Davis • Brian A. Jackson

Supported by the Office of Science and Technology Policy
and the National Institute of Justice

Science and Technology Policy Institute
RAND

The research described in this report was conducted by RAND's Science and Technology Policy Institute for the Office of Science and Technology Policy and the National Institute of Justice under contract ENG-9812731.

ISBN: 0-8330-3035-3

Cover design by Eileen Delson La Russo

Published 2001 by RAND
1700 Main Street, P.O. Box 2138, Santa Monica, CA 90407-2138
1200 South Hayes Street, Arlington, VA 22202-5050
201 North Craig Street, Suite 102, Pittsburgh, PA 15213
RAND URL: http://www.rand.org/
To order RAND documents or to obtain additional information, contact Distribution Services: Telephone: (310) 451-7002;
Fax: (310) 451-6915; Email: order@rand.org

PREFACE

An earlier RAND report, *Needs and Prospects for Crime-Fighting Technology: The Federal Role in Assisting State and Local Law Enforcement* (Schwabe, 1999), discussed various aspects of technology-related support the federal government has provided to state and local agencies and commented on needs and prospects for such support in the future. That report recommended a more exhaustive study of what law enforcement technology is currently in use across the nation and how the federal government might better render technology-related support.

Subsequently, the White House Office of Science and Technology Policy commissioned RAND's Science and Technology Policy Institute to conduct the more exhaustive study recommended by the *Needs and Prospects* report. This study was also supported by funding from the National Institute of Justice.

This report, *Challenges and Choices,* presents the overall findings of the follow-on study. A companion volume (Davis, Schwabe, and Fricker, 2001) provides more detailed findings from two nationwide surveys RAND conducted as part of the study.

The authors' aim is to provide information that may help federal policymakers in the Executive and Legislative branches as they formulate goals and programs to support technology utilization and modernization for law enforcement over the course of the first decade of the 21st century.

The Office of Science and Technology Policy (OSTP) was created in 1976 to provide the President with timely policy advice and to coordinate the science and technology investment. OSTP's Technology Division helps to develop and implement federal policies for harnessing technology to serve national goals such as global economic competitiveness, environmental quality, and national security. The Division's priorities include: sustaining U.S. technological leadership through partnerships to promote the development of innovative technologies; research and development (R&D) and policy initiatives for advanced computing and communications technologies; advancing technologies for education and training; and the U.S. space and aeronautics program.

The Science and Technology Policy Institute at RAND was created by Congress in 1991 as the Critical Technologies Institute and renamed in 1998. It is a federally funded research and development center sponsored by the National Science Foundation and managed by RAND. The Institute's mission is to help improve public policy by conducting objective, independent research and analysis on policy issues that involve science and technology. To this end, the Institute

- Supports the Office of Science and Technology Policy and other Executive branch agencies, offices, and councils
- Helps science and technology decisionmakers understand the likely consequences of their decisions and choose among alternative policies
- Helps improve understanding in both the public and private sectors of the ways in which science and technology can better serve national objectives.

Science and Technology Policy Institute research focuses on problems of science and technology policy that involve multiple agencies. In carrying out its mission, the Institute consults broadly with representatives from private industry, institutions of higher education, and other nonprofit institutions. Inquiries regarding the Science and Technology Policy Institute may be directed to:

Bruce Don, Ph.D.
Director, Science and Technology Policy Institute
RAND
1200 South Hayes Street
Arlington, VA 22202-5012
Phone: (703) 413-1100
http://www.rand.org/scitech/stpi
E-mail: stpi@rand.org

CONTENTS

FIGURES

TABLES

EXECUTIVE SUMMARY

Under the American federal system most law is cast as state statutes and local ordinances; accordingly, most law enforcement is the responsibility of state and local agencies. Federal law and federal law enforcement come into play only where there is rationale for it, consistent with the Constitution. Within this framework, a clear role has been identified for federal support of state and local agencies. A major area of such support is technology-related with activities taking the following forms:

- Sponsoring research and development (R&D),
- Testing and evaluating technology and developing performance standards for technology and its use,
- Funding and otherwise assisting with acquisition of or access to technology,
- Providing training in the use of technology and developing technology used in training,
- Providing technology assistance by applying federal technology and expertise to specific problems, and
- Providing information on technology and its use in law enforcement.

This report provides findings of a study of technology in use or needed by law enforcement agencies at the state and local level, for the purpose of informing federal policymakers as they consider technology-related support for these agencies. In addition, it seeks to characterize the obstacles that exist to technology adoption by law enforcement agencies and characterize the perceived impact of federal assistance programs intended to facilitate the process. The study findings are based on a nationwide Law Enforcement Technology Survey (LETS) and a similar Forensics Technology Survey (FTS) conducted in late spring and early summer 2000, interviews conducted throughout the year, focus groups conducted in autumn 2000, and review of an extensive, largely non-academic literature.

LESSONS FROM THE SURVEYS

Technological Lessons: Where Are We Now?

One of the main goals of the RAND Law Enforcement Technology Survey was to identify what technologies were and were not available to law enforcement organizations around the country and to gauge their future technology needs. It was to obtain an answer to the question "Where are U.S. law enforcement departments *now*?" with respect to technology. Depending on how one frames this question, a macro-level answer could simply be a more comprehensive knowledge of the range of technologies that are and are not available to local police departments. The RAND surveys can provide such an answer. When asked about their current technology capacity, respondents identified a number of technologies that were not currently available and were not "unnecessary" (LETS, 22, 25–29). This resulted in a list of potentially needed technologies from the perspective of U.S. local law enforcement. The listing of the technologies, along with the percentage of local police departments lacking them, is included in Table 1. The table is sorted in order of decreasing non-availability, down to a cutoff of 25 percent.[1]

When examining such a summary listing of unavailable technologies, it is important to place the survey responses in an appropriate context. Although the values included above are the percentages of law enforcement that indicated these technologies were both unavailable

[1]It should be borne in mind that because the surveys did not cover every current or potential law enforcement technology, this represents a limited slice of the technologies which are and are not available to local police departments.

Table 1

Technologies Not Available to Local Police

Technology	Not Available	Technology	Not Available
Detection and analysis of cyberattacks	79%	Computers in patrol cars	58%
Blister/nerve agent protective clothing	79%	Electronic listening	57%
Video conferencing equipment	75%	Night vision devices	57%
Kinetic energy projectiles	75%	Vehicles—special purpose	45%
Chemical agent detection	71%	Crowd or riot control	44%
Long-range video monitoring	69%	Computer-based training	41%
Stun devices/projectiles	68%	Conference call equipment	36%
Radioactive agent detection	66%	Computer assisted dispatching (CAD)	35%
Explosives detection	64%	Integrated data bases	34%
Polygraph equipment	64%	Protective gloves, helmets, and shields	34%
Fleeing vehicle interdiction equipment	63%	Audio-visual equipment to obtain evidence	30%
Concealed weapon detection devices	62%	Training equipment	28%
Bomb containment/ disablement equipment	60%		

SOURCE: LETS, 22, 25–29. Numbers are statistically adjusted percent of local departments reporting technology is not available.

and not unnecessary, it is likely that there is a significant barrier for a survey respondent (especially for a survey of this kind) to designate a technology as unnecessary.[2] For example, it is the case that more than two-thirds of local police departments lack "necessary" radioactive agent detection equipment (Table 1). However, the degree

[2]There is a legitimate personal and organizational interest not to refuse any resources that might improve the performance of the respondent's organization even marginally. As a result, while it is unlikely that a circumspect observer would assert that each of the 57 percent of local departments that lack night vision capability truly "need" it, there is also a clear and reasonable rationale why many survey respondents indicated that they did.

of necessity of this technology might be appropriately calibrated by considering the net increase in public safety that might accrue from providing each of these departments a Geiger counter compared to providing training equipment to the 28 percent of respondents who lacked it (or upgrading the training equipment of the many respondents who indicated that theirs was insufficient). All technology acquisition decisions, whether they are made at a local or national level, are a calculus of trade-offs and it is important to remain cognizant that there are serious consequences of losing sight of that fact.

In addition to identifying technologies that are unavailable to state and local police organizations, the RAND surveys also asked for information on the age and quality of currently available technologies. By identifying their current technologies as either obsolete or "old but serviceable," survey respondents also provided a list of technologies that may be candidates for replacement in the near-to-medium term. These responses are included in Table 2 in decreasing order of the fraction of departments characterizing them as "Obsolete" or "Old but Serviceable," down to a cutoff of 25 percent (LETS, 22, 25–29).

From the perspective of the policymaker, several things stand out from such a numerical summary of the survey results. Most striking is the fact that 18 percent—almost one in five local police departments—indicated that their administrative or accounting systems were obsolete; without such input from departments it would be difficult to see that such an "unglamorous" technology might indeed be a high priority for local police forces. Other entries on this table are less surprising. The appearance of computers and cellular telephones is not unexpected given the short product cycles and rapid obsolescence of those products. The appearance of ballistic-resistant armor (stab-resistant armor is not broadly available) on the list also holds a relevant lesson from the perspective of law enforcement technology policymaking. While bulletproof vests do "age" and become worn over time, studies have shown that the protective properties of the armor do not break down.[3] As a result, the notion of an "obsolete" bulletproof vest is a complex one likely based more on the

[3]See "Old Armor Tests As Good As New," http://www.nlectc.org/.

Table 2

Technologies in Need of Replacement by Local Police

Technology	Obsolete	Old but Serviceable	Either Obsolete or Old
Radio equipment	10%	46%	56%
Training equipment	10%	35%	44%
Administrative/accounting systems	18%	26%	44%
Computers in workspaces	7%	34%	41%
Audio-visual equipment to obtain evidence	12%	28%	40%
Crowd or riot control	12%	25%	37%
Protective gloves, helmets, and shields	9%	25%	34%
Ballistic- and stab-resistant armor	8%	25%	33%
Computer-based training	9%	20%	29%
Integrated data bases	8%	22%	29%
Conference call equipment	3%	24%	27%
Vehicles—special purpose	4%	21%	25%
Cellular telephones	2%	24%	25%

SOURCE: LETS, 22, 25–29. Numbers are statistically adjusted percent of local departments reporting as indicated.

obvious importance of the technology (and its performance) to officers rather than the technology itself.

Conceptual Lessons: Where Do We Need to Go and How Do We Get There?

These survey results are striking. There are large numbers of technologies that are unavailable to local police departments and many officers believe that the technology they have is aging and becoming obsolete. In an era when crime is becoming more and more technologically intensive, there are clearly serious technology needs in the law enforcement community. It is obvious that an important part of "where we need to go" as a nation in this area is to better outfit our law enforcement organizations with the technology they need to fight crime.

It is important, however, that consideration of these results does not stop at this level. Hasty examination of lists of "unavailable" or "aging" technologies can lead to the conclusion that the solution to the problem is to "just buy them what they need"; the assumption is made that laying out the situation "as it is now" implies only one course for how to get "where we need to go." This simplifies discussion too far because, in reality, there are many ways to approach these problems that should be considered to ensure resources are not wasted and the nation gains the greatest benefit for its investments. Reading these results as a "shopping list," for example, eliminates discussion of the important trade-offs that must be made among technologies, among what functionalities are truly "needed" by law enforcement at all levels, and the priority level of individual improvements. For example, a third of departments report that their workspace computers are "old but serviceable"; while making good computer technology available is important, the costs and benefits of upgrading all computers to "state of the art" must be weighed against the unavailable technologies above and also against other uses such as providing training to better use technologies that are already available, or performing R&D to generate the potential that superior technologies will be available in the future.

Barriers to Technology Adoption

To address these many complex considerations in a coherent way, it is relevant to consider a general framework of the many obstacles that can get in the way of an organization, in this case a law enforcement organization, adopting new technology. These barriers impact whether organizations initially choose to adopt a new technology and, after they have chosen to do so, how effectively they put the technology to use.

When considering the adoption of law enforcement technologies by local police, however, it is first important to point out that generalizing is difficult. There are significant differences among technologies that make it more or less likely that departments even want to adopt them; actual desire for a technology is a critical first "barrier" that must be passed before any more "practical barriers" matter. Rural departments, for example, were much more likely to indicate that they had no need for technologies used in crowd control. It is therefore irrelevant to discuss barriers inhibiting their adoption since pursuing undesired or unuseful technology is, by definition, counterproductive.

For technologies that are desired by organizations, however, there are serious barriers to pursuing and utilizing them. For the broad classes of technologies included in the surveys, these barriers have been broken down into four classes:

- **Costs**—including both the procurement cost of a technology and the opportunity cost of that technology compared to other uses of resources. Includes implicit trade-offs and assessments of the benefits of new techniques or equipment.
- **Technology Risk**—the risk that the technology will not perform as expected or fulfill the tasks desired of it.
- **Human Associated Risks**—the risk that the members of the organization will not be able to adapt sufficiently to the new technology so it is not put to effective use or, in the extreme case, not utilized at all.
- **Unanticipated Potential Costs**—the risk that new technology will have unintended consequences. In this context the primary unanticipated costs are in the area of liability risk or the risk of adverse public opinion associated with using a new technology.

In addition to asking survey respondents about the availability of technology, the RAND surveys also addressed these barriers to acquiring it. Of the reasons cited by respondents, cost routinely stood out as the primary obstacle to the adoption of new technologies. Such a result is not unexpected given that, at some price point, any technology becomes attractive for purchase and, until it reaches that level, cost does stand as an obvious initial obstacle to using the technology. If cost is a sufficient obstacle, none of the other barriers to adoption is relevant; if you don't have the opportunity to adopt a technology because the cost is too high, how well you adopt it is not an issue. The fact that many respondents cited cost, however, likely also represents the important and difficult trade-offs that must be made within police departments. Because of the labor intensity of their activities, technology acquisition must always compete with "placing more police on the street" or paying overtime to extend an investigator's work on a pending case. In addition, because of the variety of ways police departments could allocate their funds, trade-offs among technologies are also likely to be very important. It is not just the cost of the technology that dictates its desirability but the perceived benefits that are associated with purchase. In this light it is not surprising that fewer large urban departments cited cost for some technologies that are particularly suited to solving the problems of an urban police force.

But just as cost is clearly a barrier, other barriers to adoption are important as well. Departments are concerned about the technical risks associated with some technologies as expressed by their indicating that the "reliability/effectiveness" of the technology could be a barrier to acquisition. Smart guns stand out as such a technology where, if police departments are to adopt the technology, steps must be taken to develop it to the point where these concerns are satisfied. The human factors associated with technology adoption, as emphasized in concerns about training, training technology, and other sources of information are also clearly important for both law enforcement agencies and forensic science laboratories. The barrier that finding sufficient trained personnel poses to the effectiveness of forensic science laboratories stands as a troubling but important finding of this study. Currently, most law enforcement organizations' technology adoption efforts are less affected by concerns of unanticipated effects like public opinion. Important exceptions exist to this trend, however, including stand off and direct electrical devices, once again emphasizing the differences that exist among technologies with respect to adoption barriers.

Because of society's interest in law enforcement adopting technologies and utilizing them effectively, crafting policies that reduce barriers to adoption is of clear interest. Approaches to address these barriers have focused on several areas: provision of technical information to reduce the uncertainties associated with new technology; R&D to reduce costs, broaden capabilities, and provide new technical options; directly providing technology or funds to purchase it; and training to address the human factors of technology adoption.

Sources of Technology-Related Support and Information

To assess how these organizations were currently addressing these barriers to adoption, the RAND surveys asked about the sources of technology information and support which they regularly utilized. The most striking result in this line of questioning was the number of local departments that did not receive support from any source—on issues ranging from topics as broad as "technology testing and evaluation" to those as specific as "firearms tests." On average, two-thirds of departments never received any technology support. Of those that had received technology-related support within the past year, the primary providers of that support were:

a. In-house departments

b. Local and state agencies

c. Manufacturers and vendors.

In-house departments and local and state agencies were especially important in terms of technology-related training received by local police. Between 46 and 58 percent of local police reported receiving training support from these three sources. Not surprisingly, in-house departments were the primary source of technology-related support for many of the categories listed. State agencies provided support for trace evidence analysis to half of the respondents and to 15–25 percent of respondents for a wide range of other types of support.

Manufacturers or vendors provided support to 10–20 percent of respondents primarily in the areas of technology assistance, firearms tests, and technology testing and evaluation—in addition to support for training. Virtually all of the support for cybercrime investigations was provided either by in-house departments or local and state agencies. The majority of departments (64–83 percent) rely on trade magazines, colleagues, manufacturers, or word-of-mouth for information on law enforcement technology.

About one out of five reported usually obtaining technology information from either Law Enforcement Online (LEO) or the National Law Enforcement and Corrections Technology Centers (NLECTCs). On specific technical topics, federal sources of advice and assistance were generally consulted by 2–6 percent of local departments. The relatively low apparent utilization of federal sources, both for technology support and information, is troubling from a policy perspective given that many sources utilized by police—including manufacturers, trade magazines, and Internet resources—have no incentive to provide impartial advice and many other sources are not in a position to provide either comprehensive or technically rigorous input. It is possible that these values reflect limited awareness of the programs or the limited capacity of the programs to provide support to many departments based on their current levels of budgetary and staff support.

Views on Federal Technology Assistance

It is clear that federal programs designed to lower these barriers, whether through R&D, provision of technical information, support of training, or other activities are making some progress in making the technology adoption process easier for law enforcement organizations. Considering the views expressed by respondents who had received any of a broad range of federal technology assistance, a majority of departments and crime labs always believed that the aid had been at least "somewhat helpful." However, many fewer of the respondents (often a small minority) indicated that the programs were either "very helpful" or "essential." As a result, while the broadly positive views of federal support programs on the part of those departments that have benefited from them are encouraging, the low intensity of these views suggests that there is more that can be done to increase the relevance of the aid and advice and craft it to better serve the needs of local police. In general, respondents were more positive about federal initiatives (like supply of technology or grants of funds to purchase technology) that immediately and directly send federal resources to their organizations for use. It should be noted that the generally more positive view of federal programs by crime laboratory respondents to the survey suggest that these programs are more effectively reaching their intended audience.

The relatively modest percentages of local law enforcement departments that are currently being reached by these programs suggests that they also have the potential to more broadly serve the needs of the nation's police, provided sufficient organizational and financial resources are available. It would be counterproductive to encourage more police forces in the country to take advantage of these resources if the increase in demand would overwhelm the system and make it less effective for everyone.

BROADER POLICY CONSIDERATIONS AND ISSUES

When considering federal responses to these issues, it is important to consider policies not just in terms of the short-run but also how their long-term effects can be crafted to generate the most benefit. The programs that were viewed most positively by respondents to these surveys—direct provision of technology and transfer of federal monies to the local level for technology purchases—are uniquely short-run strategies. Although it is understandable why law enforcement practitioners, who are primarily asked to solve problems in the short term, would find the quick effects of these types of programs appealing, they may not be the best way of investing limited federal resources. Provision of money that is designated for technology support eliminates the trade-offs that must be made at the local level among competing potential uses for the resources; when a particular technology is mandated as a condition of support, even trade-offs among technologies may be eliminated.[4] While providing a technology to a police force today will generate immediate benefit (assuming that the other barriers to adoption of the technology are overcome), the return on the investment will gradually decrease over time as the system is worn out or becomes obsolete. It is possible that other programs, whose returns increase with time rather than decrease, might be better policy targets.

One example of such an increasing returns target is the provision of technical training to help overcome human barriers to technology adoption. Training of individuals has the possibility not just to improve how individuals use today's technology but improve their use of technologies in the future; the potential for trained individuals to spread their knowledge within their organizations provides the chance for increased returns on the investment even in the short

[4]It should be noted that these effects have the potential to generate significant distortion in the way that funds are used at the local level since it is the competition among different potential uses and the trade-offs among alternatives that could lead to more efficient allocation.

term. The RAND survey results and findings from interviews strongly suggest the need for increased training, including training to use technology already available or being procured. This particular topic was brought up with respect to small rural departments all the way up to a large urban department with a billion dollar budget. Respondents spoke of considerable, wasteful redundancy in training curricula. Training technology is developing rapidly on many fronts, including law enforcement. Distance learning and interactive computerized training offer promise for overcoming at least some of the obstacles (e.g., lack of time and money) agencies face in training their personnel. Because of the apparent importance of training in addressing these issues, it is considered in more detail below.

Like training, R&D can also address the technology adoption barriers of organizations, but it is a much more long-term strategy. It is only though research that new technological possibilities are discovered and current technologies are adapted and applied to the needs of law enforcement. Because of the unique characteristics of the law enforcement technology market, private firms may ignore roles in this area not taken by the public sector. The importance of research as an enabling approach to these problems—exemplified by the important advances in body armor and other technologies which outfit today's officers—point out that, even though local forces may not see immediate benefits and, as a result, may not be as supportive of these programs, they are important nonetheless. Research and development can also take as a goal not only developing new technologies but improving those which are already available; selecting a target of providing rapid, cost-effective DNA analysis capabilities could go a long way toward removing the backlogs and staff shortages that currently prevent forensic laboratories from making their full potential contribution to law enforcement. Research and development therefore likely represents a unique role for government to support work that not only lowers adoption barriers for current technologies but attempts to apply novel technologies to other needs of law enforcement as well.

Differing Needs for Technology-Related Support

In addition to considering the national level implications of technology assistance programs, policy in this area must address the differing needs of different police departments. We found significant divergence in the technology-related needs of law enforcement departments based on the size of the community and population they serve. Some of these reported differences might be simply due to the fact that larger departments have greater (and more complex) technology needs than other departments. Although these departments represent a small fraction of the total number of local police and county sheriffs' departments in the United States, they also serve a much larger fraction of the total population. Further, larger departments are more likely than smaller organizations to have officers who specialize in technology-related issues (including training and grant writing). So in this sense, one might expect that the larger departments would be receiving greater federal support than the smaller agencies. At the same time, in the areas of funding for technology acquisition, training, and access to federal technology the differences by size of department are striking. These differences suggest that perhaps alternative approaches may be required in order to ensure the necessary level access to federal support in these key areas for both large and small departments.

Small Departments

A majority of both rural and urban departments serving populations less than 25,000 indicated that acquiring technology to more effectively train personnel was a high priority. In addition, two-thirds of small urban departments also rated technology to improve command and control of operations as being a high priority. Both types of departments tended to rate standards by which equipment could be judged or certified to be a lower priority than their other technology-related needs.

Moderate-Sized Departments

Local police in urban settings serving medium-sized populations also placed a high priority on technology to improve command and control of operations. In addition, urban departments serving populations in the range of 25,000–75,000 considered information to help them make better technology-related plans and important decisions.

Large Departments and State Agencies

Urban departments serving populations of 75,000–225,000 listed as high priority a variety of technology-related needs including technology to improve command and control of operations, interoperability, and to more effectively train personnel—as well as better training on technology presently available to their department. These departments ranked standards by which to judge equipment as a relatively low priority.

Priority Needs for Technology-Related Support

The results of these survey studies also showed that some areas can be identified as particularly high technology priorities for law enforcement. As shown in Tables 3 and 4, a majority of departments gave a high priority rating to technology to more effectively train personnel and for command and control operations.

Training

How important of a limiting factor training requirements are in terms of future acquisition varied across different types of policing technologies. Approximately 10 percent of departments considered training requirements to limit acquisition or use of night vision/electro-optic devices, vehicle stopping/tracking devices, and digital imaging devices.[5] One in five local departments consider training requirements to be a factor limiting acquisition or use of digital suspect composites.

---

[5]For the LETS survey to local police, percentages have been statistically adjusted to represent the entire population. See Appendix A for a description of the adjustment methodology. For the LETS survey to state police and the FTS survey to crime labs, results are reported as unadjusted percentages.

Table 3

Local Law Enforcement Agency Ratings of Technology-Related Needs

Technology-Related Need	Percent Reporting Need as High Priority
Technology to more effectively or efficiently train personnel	59%
Technology for command and control of own agency's operations	55%
Technology for improving accountability within own agency	46%
Information to make better technology-related plans and decisions	45%
Technology for interoperability with other agencies	45%
Training to use technology available or being acquired by own agency	43%
Standards for judging or certifying equipment or other technology	26%

SOURCE: LETS, 9. Numbers are statistically adjusted percent of agencies responding as indicated.

Table 4

State Law Enforcement Agency Ratings of Technology-Related Needs

Technology-Related Need	Percent Reporting Need as High Priority
Technology for command and control of own agency's operations	86%
Information to make better technology-related plans and decisions	79%
Technology for improving account ability within own agency	73%
Technology for interoperability with other agencies	64%
Technology to more effectively or efficiently train personnel	60%
Training to use technology available or being acquired by own agency	57%
Standards for judging or certifying equipment or other technology	54%

SOURCE: LETS, 9. Numbers are percent of agencies responding as indicated. Unweighted n=15.

The importance of training requirements as limiting future acquisition decisions showed no clear trends by size of population served by local police. The exception was in terms of use of tire deflation spikes: rural departments were less likely to view training as being important—possibly as a function of lesser need for these devices. Whereas, large urban (more than 225,000) departments were more likely to view training as being important—again, perhaps reflecting greater usage of these devices by these departments. State police departments showed a similar pattern in terms of the relative importance placed on training requirements in acquisition decisions vis-à-vis different policing technologies.

Command and Control

Municipal/city police departments tended to rate as a higher priority technology for command and control of operations, for improving accountability within an agency, and computer hardware than did county police/sheriffs' departments—although none of these differences were statistically significant.

A Special Need: Forensic Labs

Because of initial findings from interviews and literature examination, a concerted effort was made to focus on forensic science capabilities. To this end the team conducted a survey to examine needs and current use. Major findings from the RAND Forensic Survey include:

- Most forensic laboratories have backlogs, due principally to lack of trained technical staff or lack of automated technology that could increase staff productivity;
- When demand for forensic analysis exceeds supply—as is frequently the case—laboratory tests necessary for criminal *prosecution* are generally more likely to be performed than those needed for thorough criminal *investigation*. In particular, tests of evidence to identify controlled substances or to determine blood alcohol levels are almost always conducted because they are needed for prosecution, while tests of blood or semen evidence in murder or rape cases *where no suspect has been identified* are

often not conducted because laboratories cannot afford to do them.

Laboratories prioritized their current needs as shown in Table 5. Additional staffing and training were emphasized in comments from many laboratory directors.

In examining this situation the RAND research team noted that research and development focused on dramatically lowering the acquisition costs of a standard laboratory suite with a specified throughput capability is a unique approach to the resource problem at the local and state level. Research and development efforts aimed at redeveloping existing systems to achieve reliability or cost goals (in contrast to performance or new scientific goals) have been successfully undertaken by other federal agencies, notably the Department of Defense.

Underrecognized Needs

As is the case for most R&D activities and "behind the scenes" product development, the final customers who purchase the resulting products are often unaware of what went into them. Consequently, it is not surprising that only about 20 percent of the departments responding to the RAND Law Enforcement Technology Survey were aware of having received any federal support in the area of R&D or

Table 5

Priorities of Forensic Labs Surveyed

Current Needs	Low/Not a Priority	Medium Priority	High Priority
Additional professional staffing	4%	17%	79%
Continuing education/training on new technologies or developments	0%	33%	67%
Additional laboratory space	17%	17%	67%
Training on technology available or being acquired	3%	41%	56%
Computerized system for tracking evidence	36%	27%	37%
System for overall laboratory management	41%	28%	31%

SOURCE: FTS, 15. Numbers are percent of laboratories responding as indicated.

commercialization. Since most local departments do not perform R&D or generally request technology commercialization aid, there is little reason for them to be aware of these programs. The focus of many burdened departments and laboratories is necessarily short term on the immediate priorities of today; as a result, the long-term focus of R&D must seem distant from their current needs.

Although local departments may not rate the importance of federal R&D, standards development, or commercialization as highly as direct funding, this should not be interpreted as "evidence against" the support of these activities. There is a real need for federal sponsorship in these areas because the law enforcement market is neither big enough nor lucrative enough to attract sufficient private sector R&D investment.

Nearly three-fourths of local police departments and 42 percent of forensic laboratories reported that they had neither received nor requested any federal assistance in the technology evaluation or standards area. This apparent lack of utilization of federal standards setting and technology evaluation services is in marked contrast to the support of these activities that was expressed by participants in RAND focus groups. As one of our sources put it, "without federal support for technology standards and commercialization, the law enforcement community is destined to continue to be disappointed by vendors who try to sell them secondhand technology originally designed for other purposes."

OVERARCHING ISSUES

Throughout our research there were a number of larger issues that came to our attention. While some of these do inform our recommendations above, they are largely beyond the scope of the study or are not explicitly addressed in our survey work. They bear mention, however, if only to help remind policymakers of the larger context, problems, and prospects of employing technology more effectively with our law enforcement departments and agencies. Among the meta issues that were identified through our interactions with the law enforcement community are the following:

Forensic Sciences. Crime laboratories are struggling to keep up with demand for their services. Substantial backlogs are not uncommon.

While most laboratories appear to be able to conduct those tests of evidence needed to support prosecutions, many labs lack the capacity to support investigations equally well. Frequently, evidence is analyzed only after a suspect has been identified.

Interoperability and Data Sharing. There is a great need for improvements in communications interoperability and data sharing among agencies. The technology for this exists and continues to be improved. Frequently what appears to have been lacking is the political will to go the extra mile to coordinate and cooperate with other agencies.

Accountability and Risk Management. Technology has a role to play in increasing accountability of law enforcement officers both to their organization's leadership and to the public. As technology makes it more *possible* for law enforcement to record interviews of witnesses and suspects, to ensure that physical evidence is properly collected and protected, and to avoid unnecessary damage or destruction of persons and property, these safeguards will become more in demand. Failure of law enforcement to keep up with technology in these areas may increase risks of both civil liability and losing criminal cases in court.

Information Security and Privacy. Technology is making possible better surveillance and monitoring, as well as more comprehensive and accessible databases, which raise concerns about information security and privacy.

Availability of Expertise. Certain expertise is in short supply and is prohibitively expensive for all but the best-resourced agencies. An obvious example is expertise in cybercrime investigation and, more generally, digital evidence analysis.

Trends in Crime. Although one cannot predict whether or how long declines in crime rates will continue, it seems reasonable to prepare for increases in electronic crime (e.g., denial of service attacks, criminal transfer of funds by electronic means, possible forgery of digital signatures, etc.), continued public fear of gun violence and certain crimes (such as home-invasion robbery), and possible domestic terrorism (which may involve chemical or biological weapons).

Public-Private Interfaces. Crime mapping and Internet technologies allow law enforcement agencies to make crime maps accessible to citizens and can be used for citizens to report crimes or hot spots. LoJack, GPS-equipped cellular telephones, and other privately purchased or leased security technologies can interface with public agencies, as can private security forces at business sites, on public streets, or in correctional facilities. To what extent should the public side of these interfaces be supported?

RECOMMENDATIONS

As a result of an integrated assessment of each of these sources of information, we present the following recommendations. They constitute what the study team believes is a reasonable, yet forward-looking set of actions for federal technology-related support of state and local law enforcement.

- To avoid wasteful spending and to ensure technology is used to good effect, we recommend that federal initiatives providing technology hardware or software include provisions for training. It appears that all too often, procurements are made under the false assumption that "somebody else" will take care of training.
- To help law enforcement agencies make more effective and less disappointing technology acquisition decisions, we recommend continuing and publicizing federal testing, evaluation, and standards setting for technologies needed by state and local agencies.
- To enhance public safety, we recommend providing data network access to all police and sheriffs' departments that have unmet needs for it. No American community—large or small—wants its officers to lack information that could have been available to recognize and apprehend dangerous criminals wanted in other jurisdictions.
- To meet the demands of investigation as well as prosecution, we recommend building forensic capability well beyond current levels. This could include providing screening-test technology to first responders, as well as increasing training, recruiting, and retaining forensic scientists. We recommend it include increased federal support of R&D of forensic science techniques and technologies. One possible focus of this R&D might be on lowering

the acquisition cost for a standard, known throughput capability suite of forensic laboratory equipment.

- To correct evident competitive disadvantages of smaller law enforcement agencies, we recommend that federal agencies make a serious effort to make it easier for rural and small urban police and sheriffs' departments with real, unmet needs, to obtain funding and other technology-related support. Although some rural and small departments may have crime rates too low to warrant more substantial investment in modern technology, other rural or small departments suffer unmet needs because they lack political clout or skilled personnel available to write grant proposals.
- As a cost-effective investment, we recommend increased federal funding of R&D of technologies that automate or otherwise increase productivity of what are presently labor-intensive or training-intensive processes. Such technology can help make high-quality law enforcement more affordable.
- To promote police accountability and to provide more objective evidence of lawbreaking, we recommend that all or most patrol cars be equipped with video cameras and wireless networked computers. Videotaping provides objective evidence useful for suspect identification and prosecution, as well as for resolving complaints of police misconduct. Rapid access to current data on stolen vehicles, outstanding warrants, etc., can reduce officer uncertainty in confrontational situations. The most practical federal role in this may be in defining or developing equipment suites or standards, rather than in funding their acquisition.
- To reduce confrontational uncertainty, risk of injury to officers and the public, as well as risk of confrontations escalating into civil disturbances or abuse of police power, we recommend continued federal support for the development, testing, and deployment of technology that can be carried in patrol cars or on officers to detect concealed weapons at a safe distance.[6]

---

[6]It is also important to note that there are significant applications for any nonportable versions of this technology that might be produced during development of patrol car or police officer models. For example, stationary devices that could detect the presence of concealed weapons could be placed in schools and airports detecting

These technology specific goals, if coupled with attention to the obstacles and challenges inherent in organizational technology adoption, could lead to more effective use of technology by law enforcement organizations nationwide which, we believe, has the potential to contribute significantly to public safety, long-run cost reduction, and justice.

---

the "arrival" of any weapons into a monitored area. Such technology, if it was made reliable and cost effective enough, could allow educational institutions in particular to devote less of their resources to security and more to the primary goal of student instruction.

ACKNOWLEDGMENTS

We especially appreciate the time and effort of several hundred people who responded to our surveys on behalf of their agencies. We are also grateful to all those we interviewed and those who participated in focus groups.

We would like to thank the Consortium of Forensic Science Organizations (CFSO)[1] for their exceptional cooperation with this study. Most notably, Barry Fisher and Kevin Lothridge provided invaluable assistance in the area of forensic science.

Robert Greenberg provided material on the background of federal technology-related initiatives assisting state and local law enforcement agencies.

George Tita conducted interviews with police and sheriffs' department officials in several cities.

We relied on Sarah Cotton for help in designing the survey instruments and managing survey operations. RAND staff members Pat Ebener, Don Solosan, Linda Daly, Tim Vernier, and Ann Deville worked on the survey instruments. Amber Schroeder, Yvonne Hung,

---

[1]CFSO members are: the American Academy of Forensic Sciences (AAFS), American Society of Crime Laboratory Directors (ASCLD), American Society of Crime Labatory Directors/Laboratory Accreditation Board (ASCLD/LAB), International Association for Identification (IAI), National Association of Medical Examiners (NAME), National Center for Forensic Science (NCFS), and National Forensic Science Technology Center (NFTSC).

April Duran, Mina Kimmerling, Eric Derghazaria, and Mary Lou Gilbert made telephone calls in support of the police survey.

Ronald Fricker oversaw survey sampling and analysis. Jenny Pace and David Klein conducted analysis of police survey data.

Several people reviewed earlier drafts of this report and offered helpful suggestions for improving it. These include: Susan Ballou, Gary Cordner, Raymond Downs, Lisa Forman, Peter Greenwood, Robert Greeves, Jerry Howell, Jack Riley, Peggy Ritchie-Matsumoto, John Stedman, and Lois Tully. What deficiencies remain are, of course, due to the authors.

LIST OF ABBREVIATIONS

ACLU	American Civil Liberties Union
ATF	Bureau of Alcohol, Tobacco and Firearms
CBRN	Chemical, Biological, Radiological or Nuclear
CCTV	Closed Circuit Television, also referred to in this report as fixed-site video
CFSO	Consortium of Forensic Science Organizations
DEA	Drug Enforcement Administration
FBI	Federal Bureau of Investigation
FTS	Forensic Technology Survey (conducted by RAND in spring-summer 2000)
ICT	Information and Communications Technology
LEAA	Law Enforcement Assistance Administration
LECTAC	Law Enforcement and Corrections Advisory Council
LEMAS	Law Enforcement Management and Administration Statistics
LETS	Law Enforcement Technology Survey (conducted by RAND in spring-summer 2000)

NASIRE	National Association of State Information Resource Executives
NCIC	National Crime Information Center
NIBIN	National Integrated Ballistic Information Network
NLECTC	National Law Enforcement and Corrections Technology Center
PSWAC	Public Safety Wireless Advisory Committee
PSWN	Public Safety Wireless Network
UCJIS	Unified Criminal Justice Information System

Chapter One

INTRODUCTION

> ...[At] a time when we have a budget surplus that enables us to make some larger investments in the future, there is no reason not to "think big" when it comes to crime technology R&D. After all, the rationale for spending on crime-fighting R&D is at least as strong as the basis for the more prominent areas of federal R&D spending. As with defense, government is the ultimate consumer of law enforcement R&D. As with medical research, the public's health and safety is at stake. As with environmental research, the problems and questions are becoming more complex and more difficult to address without a coordinated program. As with all longer-range R&D, market failures limit the amount of private investment in the field.
>
> The fact that technology alone will not solve the crime problem is hardly a reason not to invest in the area. Changes in individual and societal behavior are also needed to solve medical and environmental problems, but no one suggests that we should cease our research into new medications or environmental technologies simply because they cannot be the entire answer. [As] the DNA revolution has shown...technology can not only make law enforcement more effective, but also more fair. The deeper cause of justice is served by crime technology research every bit as much as the practical cause of safety (Boehlert, 2001).

BACKGROUND AND PURPOSE

Improving law enforcement doesn't just mean putting more police on the streets. Better law enforcement and crime fighting mean improving public safety, using economic resources wisely, and promoting a fairer and more just society. As we shall see, technology can serve to reduce public fear of and concern about crime by actually making our communities safer. Technology can also be the economical way to fight crime. Policing is both labor intensive and—because our police deserve to be well paid—it is expensive. As earlier RAND work reported, about 95 percent of a typical law enforcement agency's budget is dedicated to personnel (Schwabe, 1999, p. 31). Technology can represent an important way to leverage and magnify investments made in human resources and act as a "force multiplier." Given the capabilities of technology currently existing but not yet universally available and the very plausible promise that research and development holds for yet more effective and efficient law enforcement technology, there is real reason to expect we can become safer at lower cost. So, if technology can improve public safety and be an efficient use of resources, what about justice?

Though we Americans love what technology can do for us, there lurks in the psyche of many a fear or dread of technology as a tool of repression and control, as a means for government to invade the privacy of law-abiding people, or as a force unto itself. This represents an important trade-off for the American people: the fear of technology as a concentrator of power, in this case in the hands of law enforcement, versus the good that might be accomplished with that concentrated power. This fear of the dark side of technology has often been expressed in popular culture, for example, as the omnipresence of Big Brother in George Orwell's novel, *1984*, or as HAL, the computer without respect for human life in Stanley Kubrick's movie, *2001: A Space Odyssey*. Unfortunately, abusive use of technology—including such use by police—has not been confined to fiction.

Balancing these two opposing forces hinges on just how technology is used. While acknowledging the potential for abuse, if it is used well, technology more likely offers hope for increasing the fairness and justice of law enforcement. In the light of a lengthening string of well-publicized examples, the value of DNA testing to identify the guilty and exonerate the innocent is becoming widely known. Later in this report we comment on how crime mapping, video recording of police-public interactions, and quick access to criminal justice databases can improve not only crime-fighting effectiveness and efficiency but also police accountability.

Factors Affecting the Use of Technology by Law Enforcement

This report explores how modern technology used in the service of law enforcement may improve public safety and promote justice. It attempts to build on the efforts of our earlier work (Schwabe, 1999) and provide a more comprehensive and nuanced view of the factors which affect the ways law enforcement organizations learn about, adopt, and use potentially beneficial technologies. The primary inputs into this characterization are two nationwide surveys that were performed of police and forensic science organizations. The view of technology taken in the surveys and, as a result, in this analysis is quite broad encompassing traditional technology topics like computer access and useful gadgets like less-than-lethal weapons and also less "high profile" topics such as technologies for coordinating the management of law enforcement organizations or remote case filing.

From survey responses about the technology presently available to state and local agencies and their stated technology-related priorities, we seek to gain some insight into the factors that promote or get in the way of these organizations pursuing and using new technology. The process of technology adoption by any organization is always a difficult process involving numerous risks. These risks, which can effectively block organizations from pursing new technology or, if they do pursue it, from using it effectively include:

- **Costs**—All new technologies have associated costs that, at their most basic, must be paid out of funds in an organization's budget. Evaluating these costs is an important part of technology decisionmaking and requires a number of different trade-off assessments.
  - *Trade-Off Between the Technology and Other Organizational Investments*—Because dollars spent for technology cannot be spent elsewhere as well, the cost of a new technology must be traded-off against the cost of other resources. In the case of law enforcement organizations, which must devote a large fraction of their budgets to human resources, this trade-off can be difficult.
  - *Trade-Offs Among Technologies*—Because a number of different technologies could contribute to the goals of law en-

forcement, organizations also make judgments about which technologies they will pursue. Such assessments are, at least formally, cost-benefit calculations to determine how given technologies will contribute to public safety given the specific operating conditions of a police department.

- **Technology Risk**—The choice to use any new technology is always attended by the risk that the technology will not perform the desired tasks adequately. The risk that a technology will not measure up to expectations is ever present, even for the most technologically knowledgeable organizations. This risk, which varies among technologies and over time as new technologies become more established, can lead organizations to delay or even pass up potential investments in new techniques.
- **Human Associated Risks**—When an organization alters its operations or integrates a new technology into existing procedures, there is adjustment required on the part of its members. This adjustment, which includes learning how to use the technology, in what situations it is effective, and what other changes its use requires, can be facilitated by training programs or learned through use of the technology. If organization members are not able to make the necessary adaptations, the technology could be "incompletely" adopted and ineffectively applied. The risk of this happening can be a serious barrier to technology decisionmaking in organizations.
- **Unanticipated Potential Costs**—It is also the case that the adoption of new technologies almost always has associated, but unanticipated, costs. These costs—termed by some the "law of unintended consequences"—affect technology adoption in law enforcement as they do all other technologies. One example of such an unanticipated consequence is the public reaction to use of a technology by the police. If a use is deemed "unacceptable" in the court of public opinion, any law enforcement benefits could be outweighed by these collateral costs.

Because of society's interest in law enforcement adopting technologies which make its activities more effective, promote public safety, and advance the cause of justice, how other government activities can serve to lower these barriers to adoption is of great importance to policymakers. Conclusions regarding the ability of external programs to facilitate this process have important consequences for the challenges and choices federal policymakers face in considering technology-related support for state and local agencies over the coming decade.

HOW THE REPORT IS ORGANIZED

The report is in two parts: the first deals with law enforcement's use of technology at the state and local levels, while the second addresses federal technology-related support of state and local law enforcement agencies.

The first part is divided based on individual "mission elements" of modern law enforcement. Accordingly, Part I consists of the following chapters:

Chapter 2. Crime Prevention,

Chapter 3. First Response,

Chapter 4. Investigation and Apprehension,

Chapter 5. Forensic Analysis, and

Chapter 6. Administration and Management.

The second part is divided based on the different areas of federal involvement with local and state law enforcement agencies:

Chapter 7. Sources of Technology Related Information and Support

Chapter 8. Research, Development, and Deployment,

Chapter 9. Technology Application, and

Chapter 10. Challenges and Choices.

Each chapter is organized primarily by function. For example, within Chapter 3, dealing with the First Response mission element, the major headings are:

Situation Reporting,

Tactical Communications,

Officer Deployment,

Officer Protection,

Pursuit Management, and

Counter-Terrorism.

For each function, we discuss technologies supporting it. For example, under Situation Reporting, we describe three technologies: Emergency Reporting Systems, Non-Emergency Reporting Systems, and Mass Notification Systems. To the extent we are able to do so, for each technology we present (1) findings on what's out there, (2) views on what's needed, and (3) ideas on how to get there.

USAGE OF TERMS

This report uses the term "law enforcement agencies" to include police, sheriffs, and forensic agencies at the local, county, and state levels of government. Unless otherwise denoted, we use the term "local departments" to include police and sheriffs' departments at the county and municipal levels. Similarly, unless specifically indicated, we include in the term "state police" both highway patrol and state police departments. "Departments" refers to all police, sheriffs, and highway patrol departments at the state, county, and municipal levels. "Laboratories" include forensic laboratories operated by police, prosecutors, or other law enforcement agencies, as well as those operated by coroners and medical examiners.

We use the term "technology-related support" to include the following:

- **Funding for technology acquisition** through direct or indirect grants to state or local law enforcement agencies,
- **Federally supplied technology**, such as DrugFire, the firearms evidence analysis system, which is supplied to state and local agencies by the Federal Bureau of Investigation (FBI),

- **Access to federal technology**, which may be direct, such as to FBI fingerprint data, or indirect, such as access to another agency's federally supplied technology,
- **Advice on selecting technology**, such as evaluations of technology appearing in federal publications, Internet sites, etc.,
- **Technology news**, including news about new technology, available through federal reports, newsletters, etc.,
- **Technology evaluation or standards**, objective information, including equipment/technology performance standards, test reports, and evaluations,
- **Technology assistance**, such as science or engineering advice or support, generally involving use of federal technology to respond to help state or local agencies with specific problems,
- **Technology-related training**, such as training to use mapping software for crime analysis,
- **Technology-related conferences**, and
- **Technology R&D or commercialization**, where "commercialization" refers to actions necessary to make a technology applicable, available, and affordable to state or local law enforcement agencies.[1]

In the course of this study, RAND conducted two surveys, more fully described in the Methodology section following. In this report, the RAND Law Enforcement Technology Survey is abbreviated as LETS, and the RAND Forensics Technology Survey as FTS. Where numbers follow those abbreviations, they indicate the number of the applicable survey question; for example, if the source of data is cited as "LETS, 27b," the data represent responses to LETS question 27, part b.

Certain findings from LETS categorize local police departments as "rural" or "urban," with urban being subdivided by size of population served. Our definition of rural is based on the "Rural/Urban Continuum Code," as used by the Department of Agriculture. The

---

[1]For more examples of technology-related support, see Schwabe (1999) and Appendix B of this report.

codes form a classification scheme that distinguishes metropolitan counties by size and non-metropolitan counties by degree of urbanization or proximity to metropolitan areas. Counties with codes 7–9 were defined as rural, and all others were defined as urban. When we refer to "small departments," we mean urban departments serving populations no greater than 25,000.

METHODOLOGY

We were asked by the sponsors of the study to consider three questions: Where are we now? Where do we need to go? How can we get there?

The three questions are qualitatively different. The first—where are we now—seeks objective, factual information about what technology is available and in use. We felt the best way to get that information is the most direct way: Ask people in the law enforcement agencies what technology is available to them. Recognizing that, we developed and administered two nationwide surveys of state and local law enforcement agencies. The RAND Law Enforcement Technology Survey (LETS) was mailed to a stratified random sample of 710 local police and sheriffs' departments. Four hundred eleven responded, for a 60 percent response rate. In addition, 17 state police and highway patrol organizations were randomly drawn from the 50 states, of which 15 responded. The RAND Forensics Technology Survey (FTS) was sent to all 165 members of the Association of Crime Laboratory Directors (ASCLD) whom we judged to be heads of state and local forensics laboratories; we received 70 responses, representing 105 laboratories. Appendix A describes our survey methodology in greater detail.[2]

The second question—where do we need to go—depends more on perceptions. We knew from previous work that answers to questions of this sort can be expected to vary widely, depending on one's organizational perspective, time horizon, and experience level. Accordingly, we chose a dual-track approach: first, include questions

[2]For the LETS survey to local police, percentages have been statistically adjusted to represent the entire population. See Appendix A for a description of the adjustment methodology. For the LETS survey to state police and the FTS survey to crime labs, results are reported as unadjusted percentages.

about technology-related needs in the RAND surveys and, second, augment this with literature research, interviews, and focus groups to seek a broader perspective.

The third question—how do we get there—is, perhaps, most subjective. The RAND surveys provide information on factors perceived as limiting future acquisition or use of certain technologies.[3] Through these questions, some insights could be extracted on impediments to the adoption of certain technologies. We augmented that with interviews and feedback from people whom we have reason to believe really "know the system," as well as our own considered judgment.

We are aware that there are limitations to this methodology and to the resulting study. "Technology" and "law enforcement" are so broad that it was not feasible to research everything in detail. Since there are virtually no empirical data on causal relationships between technology and crime reduction or public safety, there is no consensus on which technology matters most. Thus, we had to use our best judgment of which technologies to research.

As mentioned, we surveyed police and sheriffs' departments and forensic laboratories. We did not survey corrections agencies nor otherwise sufficiently research their technology to warrant inclusion in this report. We were able to provide only limited information on technology related to courts; what we do provide is mostly from the perspective of police.

We are also aware that respondents to surveys vary in their understanding and appreciation of current and emerging technologies. In providing data on agencies' stated priorities we are neither judging nor verifying the wisdom of those priorities; we are merely presenting them. The surveys were sent to heads of departments and laboratories, who presumably used their best judgment in deciding who would actually fill out the questionnaire. In some cases we speculate

[3]The Law Enforcement Technology Survey considered the following factors as possibly limiting future acquisition or use of a technology: no need, cost, effectiveness or reliability, training requirements, risk or liability, and public opinion. The Forensic Technology Survey considered the following factors: no expected requirement, cost, effectiveness or reliability, training requirements, lack of trained personnel, and lack of equipment or lab space.

about the source of certain responses based on broader generalizations on organizational and human behavior.

In order to augment the survey and support analysis, the focus group research sought information bearing on three questions:

1. Viewing law enforcement as a system, the components should ideally be in balance. Considering public safety, cost effectiveness, and justice as the relevant criteria, are there important imbalances in the system? If so, which appear most amenable to correction through technology?
2. Considering findings from the RAND surveys, what do you make of them?
3. Anticipating apparent societal, technological, and criminal trends, what are the most valuable technology-related investments the federal government should make to help prepare state and local law enforcement for the coming decade?

Although these questions were not answered definitively, they were conducive to stimulating productive discussion and the insights gathered helped place the survey responses from the law enforcement organizations in a broader context.

Part I

LAW ENFORCEMENT'S USE OF TECHNOLOGY

Chapter Two

CRIME PREVENTION

From the perspective of society as a whole, the best and most useful activity that law enforcement agencies can carry out is crime prevention. If crimes are successfully (and justly) prevented before they occur, the societal costs and suffering associated with the effects of crime are completely avoided. Police carry part—but by no means all—of the responsibility for crime prevention:

> Most crime prevention results from informal and formal practices and programs located in seven institutional settings. These institutions appear to be "interdependent" at the local level, in that events in one of these institutions can affect events in others that in turn can affect the local crime rate. These are . . . communities, families, schools, labor markets, places, police, and criminal justice (Sherman et al., 1997, p. v).

Crime prevention activities are also one of the more controversial parts of police work. Because of their potential impact on a broad citizenry, such activities often raise civil liberty questions. In addition, the interdependence of all the institutions and activities that go into crime prevention make it difficult to unambiguously assess the effectiveness of any individual component. In spite of the difficulty in rigorously determining what prevents crime, several police activities are at least partially justified by the assumption that they contribute to crime prevention. Here, we discuss three such functions: surveillance, crime analysis, and offender tracking.

Primary findings and observations included in the chapter include:

- With respect to video and night vision surveillance technologies, the major barrier to acquisition identified by state and local police departments is cost. This likely reflects both the absolute costs of these technologies and the trade-offs that must be made between the benefits of these versus other investments. A much smaller number of departments cited training, technology questions, and public opinion as barriers to adoption.
- Crime mapping and geocoding of law enforcement data are performed by one quarter to just more than a third of local departments. The fraction of departments using these techniques increases with the size of the populations they serve.

SURVEILLANCE

Police surveillance is one activity justified by its potential effect on crime prevention. Proponents of surveillance claim that it prevents crime by deterrence, especially when overt surveillance activities remind potential criminals of police presence and observation. Critics contend that surveillance may simply displace crime to unobserved locations, rather than prevent it. Regardless, it is the case that if an area under surveillance becomes a crime scene, the surveillance can both alert police to the need for an operational response and/or provide evidence for subsequent criminal investigation and prosecution.

Because of the many factors involved in contact between police and private citizens, surveillance technology that transmits information to police may have significant advantages over eyewitness surveillance. Technology that records video or audio information may also be especially valuable for supporting investigation and enabling prosecution.

In this section we consider fixed-site and mobile video surveillance and night vision/electro-optical surveillance, as well as the special interest topic of technology for school safety. We discuss another surveillance technology, video cameras in patrol cars, in the section of Chapter 6 on police accountability.

Fixed-Site and Mobile Video Surveillance

The RAND Law Enforcement Technology Survey (LETS) found that 59 percent of local departments and 33 percent of state police departments make no use of fixed-site video surveillance cameras.[1] Only 3 percent of local departments and 7 percent of state police reported making widespread use of this technology. None of the rural departments reported making widespread use of it (LETS, 36c).

Similarly, the RAND survey found 69 percent of local departments and 27 percent of state police departments make no use of mobile video surveillance cameras.[2] Only 1 percent of local departments and no state police departments reported making widespread use of mobile video surveillance. None of the rural or urban departments serving populations less than 25,000 reported making widespread use of this technology.

In contrast to these data on the United States, police in the United Kingdom make much greater use of fixed-site closed circuit television (CCTV) surveillance. Throughout the United Kingdom there are more than 250,000 cameras transmitting images to police. A few U.S. cities have relatively comprehensive fixed-site surveillance coverage of selected areas. For example, Baltimore uses fixed video cameras to scan all 106 downtown intersections, while New York City has a program for 24-hour remote surveillance in Central Park, subway stations, and other public places (Brin, 1998).

When asked to identify whether these technologies were unnecessary[3] or if other factors inhibited their acquisition, most police or-

---

[1]For the LETS survey to local police, percentages have been statistically adjusted to represent the entire population. See Appendix A for a description of the adjustment methodology. For the LETS survey to state police and the FTS survey to crime labs, results are reported as unadjusted percentages.

[2]"Mobile video surveillance cameras" are those that might be used in a stakeout or hostage negotiation situation. This category does not include video cameras in patrol cars, which are discussed in Chapter 6.

[3]By selecting "Not Needed" on the survey. It should be noted that there is likely a "high barrier" to an individual indicating that a technology is not needed on a survey of this kind. Given that the introductory material indicated that the survey was intended to inform federal policymakers on the needs of local police organizations, there is both an individual and organizational disincentive to indicate that *any* tech-

ganizations did not indicate that the technology was unnecessary. Of the factors presented to the respondents, cost was seen by 69 percent of local departments as a factor limiting future acquisition and use of both mobile and fixed-site surveillance cameras. It is important to note that this judgment by the respondents likely includes all the concepts of technology cost discussed in the Introduction: the absolute cost of the systems, the trade-off between spending funds on technology versus other possible uses, and the magnitude of the perceived benefits of these technologies (with respect to their costs) compared to that of other investments.[4] As a result, the fact that rural and urban departments serving populations less than 25,000 were more likely than larger departments to cite cost as a limiting factor may be due to a lower perceived benefit of the technology to these departments in addition to their potentially tighter technology budgets. The other barriers to technology acquisition cited above—technology risk, human associated risks, and unanticipated costs—seemed less important for this technology than some others in the study. Only 7 percent of local departments reported training requirements (human risk) as limiting, 4 percent cited effectiveness or reliability of the technology (technology risk), only 1–2 percent cited public opinion, and none cited risk or liability (both unanticipated costs). State police responded similarly (LETS 36b,c).

Debate about the relative costs and benefits of these surveillance technologies can be clearly seen in the public controversy surrounding their use by police. As technology increases law enforcement's ability to gather and process information about the public, society's concern may increase about the use or abuse of technology threatening individuals' rights to privacy and freedom from unreasonable search. The American Civil Liberties Union (ACLU) has expressed concern about law enforcement use of video surveillance as "an intrusive search without a warrant and without probable cause or individualized suspicion." They question statistical claims made about the efficacy of surveillance cameras, given other variables affecting the rate of reported crime, such as better lighting or other changes

---

nology with the potential to make the local force more effective is "not needed." As a result, this likely represents an over estimate of the level of technological "need."

[4]In considering these issues it is relevant to keep in mind that *any* technology becomes attractive for adoption providing its cost (or, in economic terms, its opportunity cost) is low enough compared to other uses for funds.

made along with CCTV, as well as the possibility of crime being displaced, rather than reduced, by CCTV. They are also concerned that male operators may target women for voyeuristic reasons and that CCTV may be used to target minorities disproportionately. They are calling for state and federal laws with enforceable criminal penalties to limit the scope of CCTV use (Steinhardt, 1999).

Some critics of police use of video surveillance (CCTV) nevertheless suggest reasons for expecting the trend toward increased video surveillance to continue that are also interesting from the perspective of technology adoption by law enforcement:

> First, negative findings are crowded out by the industry and practitioner-led claims of "success" which dominate the newspapers and trade magazines.
>
> Second, as the evidence of displacement firms up, areas without CCTV will fall under increasing pressure to introduce systems as well.
>
> Third, for many towns and cities, there is an element of "keeping up with the Joneses," . . . but this is not just a matter of unjustified civic rivalry. As cities are increasingly competing to attract and keep inward investment from ever more mobile multinational corporations, CCTV is seen as part of a package of measures to attract and keep business and, therefore, jobs, in the town.
>
> Fourth, regardless of its effects on the overall crime rate, CCTV can be a very useful tool in investigating statistically rare but serious criminal offences such as acts of terrorism, murder and rape.
>
> Finally, even when CCTV is shown to have a limited impact on crime, it provides a very useful tool for the police to manage the problem of informational uncertainty and for allocating resources to incidents (Norris and Armstrong, 1999, pp. 205–206).

Although the arguments above include concern about the technology's effectiveness (and represent an example of the negative publicity that can be associated with a technology), they also introduce another concept as well. Just as adverse public opinion can result from police adopting a controversial technology, it can arise as well if police do not adopt technology that a large or influential fraction of the public believes is desirable. As a result, it can serve as a catalyst for technology adoption as well as an impediment.

Night Vision and Electro-Optical Surveillance

Among local departments surveyed by RAND, fewer than 20 percent reported using night vision or electro-optical image intensifiers, infrared (thermal) imagers, or laser rangefinders. Two to three percent reported widespread use; although these included no rural departments. At the state level, 57–64 percent of departments reported limited use of these devices; none reported widespread use (LETS, 36i,j,k).

Just as was the case for the video systems discussed above, very few departments indicated that this technology was not necessary. Only 10 percent of the respondents indicated that their department had no need for night vision capability. In assessing barriers to future acquisition of these devices, cost was cited by some 63–66 percent of the respondents for the various devices. As discussed previously, this value must be viewed with the understanding that it contains judgments about the absolute costs of the devices but also the relative benefits associated with their possession and use. As before, rural and urban departments serving populations less than 25,000 were more likely to cite cost as a limiting factor than larger urban departments. Nine to eleven percent of departments cited training requirements as a limiting factor; this suggests that the human resource issues of integrating these devices into current operations was seen as slightly more serious than for the video systems. We found no clear pattern by department size in citing training requirements as a constraint (LETS, 36i,j,k). Very few departments (2–3 percent) cited concerns about the effectiveness of the technology and essentially none (0–1 percent) cited concerns about public reaction or liability risk.

School Safety

In the one-year period from July 1, 1997 through June 30, 1998 there were 2,752 homicides and 2,061 suicides of children ages 5–19 in the United States. Only 35 of these homicides (1.3 percent) and seven of the suicides (0.3 percent) occurred at school (NCES/BJS, 2000, p. 2).

Thus, although shootings at schools have commanded national attention, it is wrong to think that eliminating young people's deaths at schools is the answer to the problems of youth homicide or suicide.

Non-fatal crime, however, is another matter entirely. The number of violent crimes against students ages 12–18 away from school is only slightly higher than those occurring at school, and thefts against the same age group occur *more* commonly at school than elsewhere (NCES/BJS, 2000, p. 5). Thus, it is the non-fatal crime (that seldom, if ever, makes the evening news) that constitutes the real school safety problem.

What security measures are schools taking and what role can law enforcement technology play in approaching these problems? In the latest data available, for school year 1996–97, 96 percent of public schools reported requiring visitors to sign in, 80 percent closed their campus for most students during lunch, 53 percent controlled access to school buildings, 19 percent had conducted one or more drug sweeps (45 percent for high schools), 4 percent conducted random metal detector checks on students, and 1 percent required students to pass through metal detectors each day. All of these measures were more prevalent in urban than rural schools (NCES/BJS, 2000, p. 137). New York City public schools, for example, have a comprehensive weapon detection program, which has deployed 191 baggage X-ray machines and 305 magnetometers (walk-through units) at 72 school sites. This operates in the context of a security system including intrusion detection, access control, CCTV, and voice communications technology (Lawrence, 2000).

A recent Education Department guide to safer schools suggests several measures for enhancing physical safety, including "Monitoring the surrounding school grounds—including landscaping, parking lots, and bus stops" (Dwyer, Osher, and Warger, 1998, p. 13). It also recommends that during a crisis there be "An effective, fool-proof communication system" and "A process for securing immediate external support from law enforcement officials and other relevant community agencies" (Dwyer, Osher, and Warger, 1998, p. 19). CCTV installations can help prevent crime at schools and identify perpetrators of crimes that do occur; however, cameras may not be used everywhere:

> Cameras may *not* be used in an area where there is a "reasonable expectation of privacy." Examples of these are bathrooms, gym locker/changing areas, and private offices (unless consent by the office owner is given). Examples of where cameras are generally acceptable are in hallways; parking lots; front offices where students, employees, and parents come and go; gymnasiums; cafeterias; supply rooms; and classrooms. The use of cameras in classrooms is often debated by teachers who want cameras for protection and teachers who do not.
>
> Audio recording is often considered to be of greater legal concern than video recording in most states. The recording of conversations is viewed as more of an invasion of privacy, as conversations often take place where the participants do not expect to be overheard (Green, 1999, p. 57).

Constant monitoring of scenes from video cameras is often an unrealistic approach to security (Green, 1999, p. 30); a more effective use of CCTV is viewing recorded tape after an incident has occurred (Green, 1999, p. 25). Although color cameras have lower resolution than black-and-white ones, color cameras are more useful for identifying perpetrators of crimes (Green, 1999, p. 32). Low quality videocassette recorders (VCR) are commonly the weakest link in school surveillance systems; VCRs of acceptable quality cost approximately $500 to $1,200 (Green, 1999, p. 57).

In a charge for the application of even more advanced technology to these problems, the Law Enforcement and Corrections Technology Advisory Council (LECTAC)[5] Information Systems Subcommittee has

---

[5]LECTAC is an advisory organization to the National Law Enforcement and Corrections Technology Center (NLECTC) system, a program of the National Institute of Justice's Office of Science and Technology." LECTAC was created to identify law enforcement and corrections equipment and technology needs, and to recommend program priorities. Council members of LECTAC represent federal, state, and local criminal justice agencies; labor organizations; and national and international law enforcement, corrections, and criminal justice organizations and are appointed based on their distinguished service records.

LECTAC works to strengthen links between the National Institute of Justice (NIJ) and the law enforcement and corrections community by reviewing and analyzing the present and future technological needs of the criminal justice system, particularly at the state and local levels. It also recommends research and development priorities to NIJ, and advises the NLECTC on equipment testing and the creation of standards, user guidelines, and technical reports.

called for a review of "the role of GIS/GPS (Geographic Information Systems/Global Positioning Systems) in criminal justice and school safety initiatives, including crime mapping" (LECTAC, 2000, p. 38). Although these approaches do represent ways of addressing school security, the deployment of technology by school systems faces the same trade-offs and barriers as technology adoption by law enforcement. It is also important to keep in mind that, unlike in law enforcement where technologies are traded off against each other based on how they *contribute* to the primary public safety mission of the agency, the budget trade-offs schools face in this area must balance security technology needs *against* the primary educational purpose of their organizations.

CRIME ANALYSIS

Analysis of crime data can reveal patterns that are helpful not only in preventing and operationally responding to crime but also in increasing accountability to police leadership and the public.[6] Most departments do some type of crime analysis, most commonly preparation of crime statistics. A recent survey found:

> The majority of the departments surveyed engage in some form of crime analysis with most (73 percent) conducting analyses to fulfill Uniform Crime Report (UCR) requirements and approximately half (52 percent) calculating statistical reports of crime activity (Mamalian and LaVigne, 1999).

Although calculation of basic crime statistics is an important part of these analyses, their application to operational police work is somewhat limited. To truly provide leverage to police activities, such in-

---

LECTAC reviews the programs of the entire NLECTC system and recommends how to improve program relevance to state and local law enforcement and corrections needs. The Council collaborates with NLECTC and OLES to provide technical assistance to manufacturers and the criminal justice system. The Council also reviews and comments on draft publications, participates in ad hoc committees established by NLECTC to provide guidance on technical and policy issues, drafts articles for applicable publications, and makes presentations to peer groups to promote awareness of NLECTC programs and activities.

[6]For the interested reader, Gottlieb, Arenberg, and Singh (1994) provide a thorough primer on crime analysis and how to utilize it.

formation on crime incidence must be represented geographically. This representation, which can be done as simply as placing pins in a map, is now often performed by sophisticated mapping software. An informal poll conducted by the International Association of Chiefs of Police (IACP) found that 30 percent of respondents indicated they have used mapping software; however, those polled (members of the IACP's Law Enforcement Management Information Section) "are among the more active users of computer technology; thus, a similar survey of a random sample of all police departments in the country would likely indicate a lower percentage of departments using mapping software" (Rich, 1995, p. 3). In fact, a random sample survey conducted in 1997–98 found only 13 percent of departments using any computerized crime mapping (Mamalian and LaVigne, 1999).

The technology for crime mapping and analysis is continually improving, and law enforcement agencies are learning better ways to use it:

> Merging jurisdiction maps with crime and arrest data is transforming crime analysis from crime counts to assessments of types of crime in time and space.
>
> With the new computer software, precinct- and street-level reporting are changing how police deal with crime. District commanders are required to use changing profiles of crime in their progress reports and strategic plans. Precinct captains and shift commanders are required to review and comment on the previous day's crime maps. For the first time, officers in each new shift, as they hit the streets, know what happened during the previous shift (O'Connell, 1998, p. 87).

Whether computerized or not, data geocoding and mapping is being done by many departments, especially those serving larger urban populations. Among local police, calls for service and incidents are the most common types of data geocoded and mapped (LETS, 24). According to the RAND survey, 23 percent of local departments use some crime mapping and analysis for command review and operational planning. As would be expected, the fraction of departments for which these activities are formal (and, presumably, computerized) increases with the size of the population served by the police force (LETS, 21).

Hate crime monitoring is another potentially technology-dependent facet of crime analysis. The RAND survey found that 27 percent of state police have computerized hate crime monitoring systems, while only 10 percent of local departments have them (LETS, 16c).[7]

OFFENDER TRACKING

Interviewees and focus group participants supporting this study painted a pessimistic picture of offender-based tracking systems in use around the country. Most such systems are between 20 and 30 years old and, like most legacy systems, are now difficult to use and maintain. It is relevant to note that this also represents a situation where public opinion and liability risk may represent a factor encouraging rather than discouraging technology adoption. Victims of crime perpetrated by offenders turned loose in communities without being adequately tracked are beginning to bring lawsuits against state agencies for not having or effectively providing information that could have potentially prevented crime. As the head of corrections in one western state is said to have asked his legislators, "are you more worried about the 15,000 people I've got behind bars or the 55,000 people I have out in your communities?"

Although not directly addressed by RAND's survey instrument, these systems also represent an important technology problem for law enforcement. Better technology for offender tracking has the potential to increase public safety by making information on offenders easier to share and utilize. It should be noted, however, that such systems raise many of the same civil liberties issues discussed above vis-à-vis video surveillance. As a result, they represent another case where the use of a technology by law enforcement must be balanced against individual rights and the resulting (potentially conflicting) public perceptions of the activity.

---

[7]It should be noted that the survey instrument did not, for these particular technologies, ask respondents to rate the priority, usefulness, or impact of these sorts of systems.

Chapter Three

FIRST RESPONSE

In spite of well-intentioned and rigorously pursued prevention efforts by law enforcement and others, a certain amount of crime will likely always occur. When criminal acts do happen, the focus of law enforcement shifts to finding the most effective ways and methods to respond. In this chapter, the process of police response is broken down into the broad areas of situational reporting, tactical communication, protection of officers, and management of pursuit. The chapter concludes with a discussion of the special interest topic of counter-terrorism.

Major findings from the chapter include:

- Command and control technology is considered a high or medium priority by 93 percent of both state and local law enforcement organizations. Not unexpectedly, larger urban departments felt this was a higher priority than smaller or rural departments.
- Although state police agencies rated communications interoperability as a higher priority than local departments, 87–92 percent of both types of departments rated it at least of medium priority.
- When police department representatives were queried about a number of less-than-lethal weapons and other technologies, they identified a number of roadblocks to their future acquisition and deployment. Primary among these was cost, likely reflecting both the cost of the systems and the trade-offs that are involved in funding technology versus other uses of funds. Training, techno-

logical risk, and potential liability/public opinion were also cited for some but their impact varied among technologies.

SITUATION REPORTING

Before police agencies can respond to a crime in progress or the aftereffects of criminal activity, they must become aware of what is happening within their jurisdiction. As a result, characterizing the assets that are available to these organizations for situational reporting is an important first step in the analysis of their technological needs.

Emergency Reporting Systems

911 systems provide a means for the public to report emergencies to the police. Availability of 911 systems has steadily increased over the years for which data are available. As Figure 1 shows, most local departments now have enhanced systems, which can automatically identify the location of a caller.

Not unexpectedly, urban departments serving larger populations are the best equipped, with most having enhanced 911 systems. Rural departments are the least well equipped, with more of the basic 911 systems and fewer of the enhanced ones. Fifteen percent of rural departments do not have any 911 system. One-third of state police have enhanced 911 systems, and another one-third have basic systems (LETS, 14).[1,2]

Only 2 percent of local and none of the state departments responding to the RAND Law Enforcement Survey characterized their 911 systems as obsolete. Twenty-three percent of local departments said

---

[1]It is interesting to note that urban departments serving populations between 75–225K appear to be slightly better supplied with 911 systems than those serving the largest cities. From the LETS survey, 96 percent of the 75–225K city departments have enhanced systems, 3 percent have basic systems and only 1 percent lack a system. Of the largest city departments, 84 percent have advanced systems, 12 percent have only basic systems and 4 percent lack a system (LETS, 14).

[2]For the LETS survey to local police, percentages have been statistically adjusted to represent the entire population. See Appendix A for a description of the adjustment methodology. For the LETS survey to state police and the FTS survey to crime labs, results are reported as unadjusted percentages.

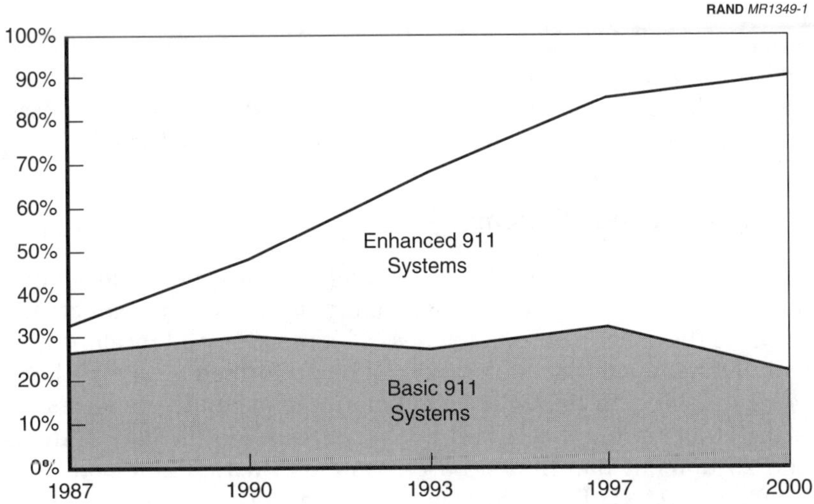

SOURCE: Reaves and Goldberg, 2000, p. 10; LETS, 14; Values reported from LETS are statistically adjusted percent of local police departments.

Figure 1—Percent of Local Police with 911 Systems

their systems were old but serviceable, and 66 percent described theirs as modern or state of the art. Seventeen percent of state police described their systems as old but serviceable, and 58 percent said theirs were modern or state of the art (LETS, 22a).

Non-Emergency Reporting Systems

In addition to 911 systems, a number of other reporting systems can serve to promote situational awareness on the part of police organizations. One such system is a three-digit, non-emergency reporting system. The RAND survey found that 7 percent of local departments have three-digit, non-emergency phone call systems, with municipal police departments accounting for 6 percent and county police or sheriffs' departments only 1 percent (LETS, 15).

More commonly, departments have one or more hotlines to deal with specific law enforcement problems. The most prevalent type of hotline is for reporting domestic violence, such as spousal, child, or elder abuse. Municipal departments are twice as likely as county police/sheriffs' departments to have hotlines. Other types of hotlines include those for reporting graffiti, gun tips, gangs, teens, homeless, and environmental accidents/natural disasters (LETS, 15d,e,f).

Mass Notification Systems

In the event of a major emergency that requires mobilization of a large fraction of the police force, technological systems can greatly increase the speed and effectiveness of contacting and recalling officers. Such mass notification tasks can be performed by either phone or fax machine. In 1997, 10 percent of municipal police departments with 100 or more officers had fax-based mass notification systems and 23 percent had phone-based systems (Reaves and Goldberg, 1999). The RAND Police Survey, performed three years later, indicated that 11 percent of municipal police departments of all sizes have fax-based systems, and 23 percent have phone-based systems. Thus, we found no evidence of growth in these types of systems over the past few years (LETS, 15b).

TACTICAL COMMUNICATIONS

In the management of evolving police operations under often-dangerous conditions, clear and effective communication between officers and their leaders is critical. Without the ability to rapidly convey information and intelligence about circumstances and activities, it is impossible to position officers and other resources efficiently and could result in injury or loss of life to both public servants and private citizens. As a result, communications is an area of great technological importance for law enforcement activities.

Communications Within Agencies

Because of the geographic area over which all police departments must spread their resources, it is obvious that facile intra-agency communication is essential for operational effectiveness and coordination of department activities. According to the RAND survey, virtually all police departments have high-quality radios available

(LETS, 22l). Most local departments also have cellular telephones available to support their operations. Only 14 percent of local departments indicated that cellular telephones were not available; 60 percent of departments indicated that their systems were modern or state of the art (LETS, 22c).

A recent study conducted by the National Law Enforcement and Corrections Technology Center, Rocky Mountain Region, found that most state and local law enforcement agencies (73 percent) currently have conventional analog communications systems that operate in high VHF bands; however, by 2007, agencies operating in 800 MHz are expected to grow from 23 to 51 percent, those using digital systems are expected to increase from 13 to 25 percent, and organizations using trunked systems are expected to increase from 24 to 27 percent (Taylor, Epper, and Tolman, 1998, pp. ix–x). Such a shift implies a significant demand for new technology in this area and a significant amount of technology adoption activity.[3]

In order to assess the perceived need for these types of technologies among local and state departments, the RAND survey asked respondents to rate their need for technology for command and control of their agency's operations as high, medium, or low/no priority. Overall, 55 percent of local departments rated this as high priority, 38 percent as medium priority, and only 7 percent as low/no priority. Among state police the percentages were 75, 17, and 8, respectively (LETS, 9b).

The RAND survey found major differences in perceived need for command and control–related technologies between rural and urban departments. Urban departments of all sizes were about twice as

[3]The integration of command and control technology into the fundamental processes of police department operation can be especially challenging. Examples of information sources intended to facilitate this process include the recent publication by Imel and Hart (2000) of an in-depth guidebook on wireless communication technology and issues for law enforcement planning and management. Additional information on communications technology and on funding communications projects can be found at the web site of the Public Safety Wireless Network (PSWN), www.pswn.gov. The vision of PSWN is for seamless, coordinated, and integrated public safety communications for the safe, effective, and efficient protection of life and property. Improving interoperability and public safety communications is seen as a multidimensional challenge, taking into account spectrum, funding, technology, organization, and operations.

likely as rural departments to consider this need a high priority. Nearly one-fifth of rural departments indicated that technology to improve command and control was a low priority or not a priority for their agency (LETS, 9b). This most likely reflects the greater complexity of managing the operations of the larger urban departments.

Interoperability Among Agencies

The Law Enforcement and Corrections Technology Advisory Council (LECTAC) Communications Subcommittee has identified interoperability as its highest priority. As a result, it has recommended that any future funding for interoperability of law enforcement and corrections follow the PSWAC[4] regulations and system guidelines and not be tied to manufacturers (LECTAC, 2000, p. 31).

The study cited in the previous section by Taylor et al. has also provided strong evidence for the need for interoperability among agencies. They found that agencies of *all* sizes and types need interoperable communications, "with 93 percent interoperating on a daily or weekly basis with local organizations, 63 percent interoperating with state-level organizations daily or weekly," though only 15 percent interoperate with federal organizations daily or weekly (Taylor, Epper, and Tolman, 1998, p. x). The authors went on to say that "agencies of all sizes and types identified limitations in funding and different bands as the two biggest obstacles to interoperability" (Taylor, Epper, and Tolman, 1998, p. xi).

The RAND survey asked respondents to rate their need for technology for interoperability with other agencies as high, medium, or low/no priority. The state police respondents ascribed the greatest importance to interoperability with 67 percent indicating it was a high priority, 25 percent a medium priority and only 8 percent as low or not a priority. For the local organizations, interoperability was seen as somewhat less important with 45 percent identifying it as high priority, 42 percent as medium priority, and 13 percent as low/no priority (LETS, 9b).

---

[4]The final report of the Public Safety Wireless Advisory Committee (PSWAC) to the Federal Communications Commission can be downloaded from http://www.pswn.gov/pswac.htm.

OFFICER DEPLOYMENT

Because of the complexity in matching police resources to the evolving needs of a jurisdiction, technology can have a role to play in helping to effectively dispatch officers and department assets. The RAND survey found that 61 percent of local police departments have Computer Assisted Dispatching (CAD) systems; however 37 percent of local police departments and 44 percent of county sheriffs' departments do not have a CAD system available to their department. Local police departments were twice as likely than county sheriffs' departments to indicate that the quality of their CAD systems was either obsolete or old but serviceable. About half of rural and urban departments serving populations less than 25,000 did not have a CAD system available to them. Of the 39 percent without CAD, about a third reported no need for it (LETS, 22d).

Among local police with CAD systems, its availability and overall quality differ by size of department. Departments in larger urban areas are more likely to have modern or state-of-the-art CAD systems than rural or small urban departments (LETS, 22d).

We found that a third of state police do not have a CAD system available to them. Sixty percent of state departments rated their CAD systems as being old but serviceable or modern/state of the art (LETS, 22d).

OFFICER PROTECTION

Weapons and Personal Protection Devices

Law enforcement officers use weapons and various personal protection devices to deter or suppress violent criminal acts and to protect themselves, the public, and criminals themselves from avoidable violence and injury.

Lethal Weapons

Because of the inherent danger associated with criminal justice activities and responding to violent crime, deployment of service handguns and other lethal weapons is an important part of most departments' officer protection programs. The Bureau of Justice

Statistics (BJS) 1997 Law Enforcement Management and Administrative Statistics (LEMAS) study found that 94 percent of local police departments and 95 percent of sheriffs' departments authorized use of some type of semiautomatic sidearms. This was a substantial increase since 1993, when the figures had been 84 percent and 82 percent, respectively. In 1997 two-thirds of both local police and sheriffs' departments authorized use of the 9mm semiautomatic, more than half authorized use of the .40-caliber and .45-caliber semiautomatics, while less than 20 percent authorized .38-caliber and 10mm weapons. Sixty-two percent of local police and 64 percent of sheriffs' departments supplied sidearms to officers (Reaves and Goldberg, 2000, p. 20; Goldberg and Reaves, 2000, p. 21).

Less-Than-Lethal Weapons

Because of the reasonable desire to limit injury to suspects, officers, and other citizens, lethal force is always viewed as the most serious response to public safety situations. As a result, in an effort to provide other options to officers, research has been directed toward developing alternate technologies and techniques. "Less-than-lethal" has come to be the preferred term for protection devices that are, somewhat optimistically, referred to by the public as "non-lethal." More conservatively, some police officers refer to them as "less lethal" weapons. Regardless of the term used, these weapons and devices are intended to allow officers to take control of confrontational individuals and unstable situations without needing to resort to deadly force. This is desirable both from humanitarian and risk management perspectives.

For many years the most commonly used less-than-lethal weapon has been the baton. More recently, the collapsible/expandable baton has been gaining favor over the traditional or side-handled varieties. Pepper spray (OC)[5] has come into common usage as a chemical

---

[5]OC is an abbreviation for Oleoresin Capsicum, a product derived from various peppers. OC is an inflammatory agent that works upon contact, causing a very painful burning sensation in the eyes, nose, mouth, and throat, making it very difficult, for someone who has been sprayed, to do the simplest of functions.

agent that can subdue individuals without undue harm. CS[6] and CN[7] gases are chemical agents that are far less commonly used.

Table 6 compares responses in 1997 when LEMAS asked if local departments authorized use of various LTL devices to responses in 2000 when LETS asked local departments to describe their use of the same devices as "not in use," "limited use," or "widespread use." What we see is that, although a substantial minority of local departments now make limited use of CN, CS, and flash/bang grenades, very few make widespread use of these devices. Capture nets are scarcely used at all.

Similar to the situation in local police departments, batons (especially collapsible/expandable ones) and pepper spray are in widespread usage among state police. Other types of gas/chemicals and crowd/riot control devices are in limited use by state police

Table 6

Types of LTL Weapons Authorized or in Use by Local Departments

Device or Agent	Authorized by Local Police, 1997	Authorized by Sheriffs, 1997	Limited Use by All Local, 2000	Widespread Use by All Local, 2000
Traditional baton	46%	38%	26%	19%
Side-handled baton	47%	36%	17%	15%
Collapsible/ expandable baton	61%	59%	25%	53%
OC (pepper spray)	89%	87%	12%	76%
CN (tear gas)	3%	3%	23%	3%
CS	4%	4%	22%	2%
Capture net	—	1%	1%	—
Flash/bang grenade	11%	19%	26%	1%

SOURCE: Reaves and Goldberg, 2000, p. 21; Goldberg and Reaves, 2000, p. 22; LETS, 31. Values from LETS are statistically adjusted percent of local departments indicating each level of use for individual LTL technologies.

---

[6]CS, an abbreviation for O-chlorobenzylidene malonontrite, causes severe eye irritation, a profuse flow of tears, skin irritation (especially on moist areas of the body) and irritation of the upper respiratory tract, causing sneezing, coughing, and difficulty in breathing.

[7]CN is an abbreviation for Chloroacetophenone, commonly called tear gas, which causes profuse tearing, an intense burning sensation to the face, and disorientation.

departments. Handheld electrical devices and flash/bang grenades were more common among state police than local police—though their usage was limited.

Because of the inherent danger in the situations police officers face in the line of duty, less-than-lethal techniques must be considered carefully; while there are good reasons to provide officers with options in responding to situations, it is important to understand how the use of those different options may change the risk posed to officers in the line of duty. Although risk comparisons between lethal force and non-lethal force are difficult, examinations have been made among less-than-lethal technologies. In one study, for example, technological LTL technologies like chemical sprays were compared with "lower tech" responses like basic bodily force (Meyer, 1991). This examination found that the TASER and chemical irritant sprays were safer and about as effective as any of several other LTL weapons or tactics (Table 7).

In an effort to gauge the barriers to police departments acquiring these technologies, the RAND Police Survey addressed both department requirements and barriers to future acquisition of LTL devices or products. Looking across different categories of less-than-lethal devices, roughly a quarter to a third of local police indicated no future requirement for these types of devices. These values could reflect both departments that already have the technologies and therefore see "no need" for future acquisition in addition to departments that lack the technology but do not desire it. In terms of other factors that might limit future acquisition decisions, local police cited:

- Cost, training requirements, and liability rated as the top three factors cited in terms of limiting future acquisition or use of these technologies.
- Cost showed the greatest variability among the different categories of less-than-lethal devices or agents in terms of the percentage of local police that viewed it as being an important limiting factor. Between 25 and 30 percent of local police rated cost as an important limiting factor for crowd/riot control devices and individual apprehension devices. In contrast, for batons—which

Table 7

Safety and Effectiveness of LTL Weapons and Tactics

Weapon or Tactic	Major or Moderate Injuries to Suspect	Major or Moderate Injuries to Officer	Successful in Ending Altercation
Baton	61%	16%	85%
Karate Kick	20%	11%	87%
Punches	64%	36%	75%
Miscellaneous Bodily Force	46%	15%	94%
Flashlights	80%	4%	96%
Swarms	24%	16%	92%
TASER	0%	0%	86%
Chemical Irritant Sprays (CS and CN)	0%	0%	90%

SOURCE: Meyer (1992, pp. 13–14).

are standard police equipment—cost was rated as being an important limiting factor by only 5–10 percent of local police.[8] In addition to reflecting the differences in absolute cost of the different technologies, these cost judgments contain implicit assumptions about the benefits of the technologies.

- Not unexpectedly, training requirements varied markedly among the different technologies as a barrier to adoption. They were highest for flash/bang grenades (22 percent) and blunt trauma/soft projectiles (20 percent) and lowest for traditional batons (11 percent) and other chemical agents (8 percent).
- About 1 out of 20 local police rated public opinion as a limiting factor for most LTL. This factor was especially important for handheld electrical devices where more than 1 in 10 cited it as a reason.
- Concern about the effectiveness or reliability of the technologies was cited by a small number of local departments and ranged from 2 percent (for flash bang grenades) to 8 and 9 percent (for handheld electrical device and traditional batons) (LETS, 31).

[8]Not surprisingly, since batons are in common usage.

The RAND survey found that factors considered important in terms of future acquisition decisions for less-than-lethal devices vary by size of department as measured by size of population served. Overall, urban police serving larger populations are more likely to expect future requirements for gas/chemical agents, individual apprehension devices, and flash/bang grenades. Except for pepper spray and traditional batons, larger departments across the various categories of less-than-lethal devices and agents tended not to view cost as being an important limiting factor influencing future acquisition decisions. This could reflect the greater absolute resources of these departments or a greater perceived benefit of the technologies to their operational needs.

Larger departments tended to be less likely to consider training requirements to be limiting use of batons. This suggests that the human factors associated with technology adoption could be more problematic for small police forces that, because of their smaller pool of officers and staff, may make learning and assimilating new technologies more difficult.

Potential unanticipated consequences of adopting these technologies also seem to be more important for larger departments. While larger departments are less likely to view liability or risk as a limiting factor with respect to the use of batons, they are more likely to view risk as being a limiting factor with respect to the use of handheld electrical devices (stand-off only) and flash/bang grenades. In addition, larger departments are also more likely to view public opinion as an important factor when considering future acquisition decisions with respect to gas/chemicals, handheld electrical devices (direct contact and stand-off), and flash/bang grenades.

Larger departments also seem to have a greater sensitivity to technological risks of these technologies, possibly because of the broader scope/higher stakes of many of their operations. Across most categories of less-than-lethal devices and agents, larger departments are more likely to consider effectiveness or reliability of the device as an important factor limiting future acquisition decisions.

Body Armor

Because of the use of firearms in criminal activities, shielding of police officers via body armor is an important part of force protection. In 1997, 43 percent of local police and 39 percent of sheriffs' departments required that all field/patrol officers wear body armor while on duty. Eighty-one percent of local police and 85 percent of sheriffs' departments supplied protective body armor to at least some of their regular field officers. In departments of all sizes, use of body armor has steadily increased since 1990 (Reaves and Goldberg, 2000, p. 20; Goldberg and Reaves, 2000, p. 21).

In the RAND survey, survey respondents were asked about the availability of ballistic- and/or stab-resistant armor and, if it was available, to rate its quality as state of the art, modern/little room for improvement, old but serviceable, or obsolete. A large majority of local police officers have access to body armor; only 9 percent indicated that it was not available. A majority of those with armor available (58 percent) responded that their available armor was modern or state of the art; the remainder (33 percent) characterized their armor as old but serviceable or obsolete (LETS, 25a). Such a response is interesting because the technology of commercially available body armor has not markedly improved in recent years and, furthermore, studies have demonstrated that the actual protective properties of armor do not degrade over time. It is also the case that stab-resistant armor has only recently begun to come on the market so it is not yet in wide use. As a result, this response should not be interpreted to mean that these police are at greater risk because of the age of their body armor but rather as a demonstration of both the importance of this technology to officers and the large likely payoff to research and development that can improve the performance (and comfort) characteristics of these products.

Smart Guns

"Smart guns" are firearms equipped to prevent firing by unauthorized people. The rationale behind their design and production is to increase firearm safety. Several rationales for smart gun development have been offered including:

- Reduction in numbers of police and corrections officers shot by criminals gaining access to the officers' firearms;
- Reduction in numbers of accidental or intentional shootings by children, youth, or others gaining access to adults' weapons; and
- Reduction in numbers of thefts of guns (if stolen smart guns were unusable).

The federal government has funded smart gun development; however, to date, reliability of prototype models has been questioned. Design requirements for smart guns are rather stringent, including the need to be usable in either the right or left hand. Present semi-automatic handguns probably cannot be retrofitted as smart guns, but there is a possibility that "smarts" could be retrofitted into revolver handgrips. Some smart gun concepts would call for electronic detonation of special ammunition, which would presumably be more expensive than common bullets with conventional primers.

Cost is the most commonly cited factor limiting future acquisition of smart guns by state and local law enforcement agencies (LETS, 36q). Given that these firearms are not yet on the market, this cost concern must be interpreted either as a perception of their likely cost or a judgment that the money that could be spent on smart guns would be better invested elsewhere. Some people we interviewed see a greater potential for smart gun use by corrections employees than by police officers.

The LECTAC Law Enforcement Operations Subcommittee has viewed the smart gun as "more oriented to the civilian market than law enforcement" (LECTAC, 2000, p. 40), while the Weapons and Protective Systems Subcommittee favored continued development of a smart gun "in spite of serious concerns about product reliability" (LECTAC, 2000, p. 44). These technological uncertainties are also clearly reflected in the survey results (Table 8).

The fraction of departments expressing concern about the training required to use smart guns is comparable to or higher than many of

Table 8

Factors Limiting Future Acquisition or Use of Smart Guns

	No Need	Cost	Effectiveness/ Reliability	Training	Risk	Public Opinion
Local police	19%	46%	14%	10%	5%	1%
State police	0%	47%	20%	20%	7%	0%

SOURCE: LETS, 36q. Numbers are statistically adjusted percent of departments indicating that their future acquisition or use is limited by factor shown.

the other technologies in the survey. This suggests that the organizations have concerns about the adjustment that will be required by their officers if they chose to pursue the technology. This is notable given that firearms in general are arguably one of the most completely and effectively adopted technologies by law enforcement and the addition of user-recognition technology could be considered an incremental change to the basic firearm design. More striking than the departments citing training, however, is the level of concern about the effectiveness and reliability of the technology. The numbers observed for smart guns (14 percent among local police and 20 percent among state departments) are the highest for any technology in the survey. This suggests that there will be a high barrier to adoption of these firearms by law enforcement until further R&D demonstrates their effectiveness and reliability.

Drug and Weapons Detection

The LECTAC Contraband and Detection Subcommittee has identified its top priority for law enforcement the development of an improved "handheld weapon, drug, and currency detector that is affordable, easy to use, rugged, reliable, and portable (LECTAC, 2000, p. 32). These desirable characteristics have been echoed by similar committees concerned with problems and challenges in the management of correctional facilities. Having a reliable ability to detect concealed weapons before confronting a person at close quarters would greatly assist police and security guards in enforcing laws and ensuring safety of officers, the public, and suspects.

Sherman et al. (1997, pp. 8-30 to 8-32) has suggested that proactive arrests for carrying concealed weapons via directed police patrols in gun crime hot spots and better methods for discovering weapons during traffic enforcement and field interrogations as promising means to reduce gun crimes. Advances in law enforcement technology could facilitate both approaches. Technologies offering promise in this area include magnetic resonance devices, acoustic devices, and edge detection radar.

PURSUIT MANAGEMENT

Because of the high profile and high risk associated with vehicle pursuit, technologies to make automobile chases more manageable (or avoid the need for direct pursuit) could be very useful to law enforcement. The top priority recommendation of the LECTAC Law Enforcement Operations Subcommittee is for vehicle stopping, including "run flat" tire effort (LECTAC, 2000, p. 39). At the current time, respondents to the RAND Police Survey indicate that use of vehicle stopping and tracking technologies by local police departments is quite limited. When asked about the general category of "fleeing vehicle interdiction equipment," most respondents (69 percent) indicated that none was available to their department (LETS, 26a). When asked about specific technologies, the results were essentially analogous (Table 9).

State police reported on average limited-to-widespread use of tire deflation spikes. However, they indicated either no use or limited use of tracking devices.

Not unexpectedly, use of vehicle stopping and tracking technologies differed among different categories of police departments. Tire deflation spikes are twice as likely to be used by urban departments serving more than 25,000 than by rural or smaller urban departments. Furthermore, none of the rural or smaller urban departments responding to the RAND Law Enforcement Survey have stolen vehicle-tracking technology, such as LoJack. No more than 11 percent of the larger departments have it.[9] These differences likely

[9]LoJack represents an interesting case where the availability of a technology to local police is independent of the departments' decisionmaking processes. LoJack provides

Table 9

Use of Vehicle Stopping/Tracking Technologies by Local Police

Device	Not in Use	Limited Use	Widespread Use
Tire deflation spikes	67%	18%	15%
Stolen vehicle tracking (e.g., LoJack)	86%	12%	2%

SOURCE: LETS, 36m,o. Numbers are statistically adjusted percent of departments responding as indicated.

reflect differences in need for the systems in addition to access to them.

The RAND survey found that cost was highlighted as an important factor in limiting future acquisition of vehicle stopping or tracking devices, indicating that they did have concerns both about the absolute and relative costs of these technology.[10] In addition to cost, other factors also came into play as well. Local police considered reliability, training, and risk or liability as limiting acquisition (LETS, 36).

Rural and urban departments serving populations less than 25,000 were more likely to cite cost as a limiting factor; this could reflect that other uses of those resources are simply perceived as more appealing based on the assumed payoff of the technologies. It is relevant to remember that at a low enough cost, any technology becomes attractive. The larger the population served by a department, the more likely factors such as reliability, training, and risk or liability as being important. This is consistent with the fact that these departments would likely have a greater assumed payoff from the technologies (since they would likely use them more frequently) and

---

the receiving units to police departments free of charge in areas where it wishes to offer its car recovery transmitters to customers. As a result, the availability of this technology to departments is more dependent on LoJack's business model than local choice.

[10]It is puzzling that 55 percent of respondents indicated that cost was a barrier to adopting vehicle recovery systems since, in the case of LoJack, the technology is provided free of charge to police departments. This result may reflect concern about associated costs or simply reflect the other concepts of costs discussed in this report—that the relative benefits of this technology may not by high for some departments. This is not inconceivable for many very small or rural police agencies.

would be more concerned about the more operational facets of adopting the devices.

For electrical/engine disruption[11] and stolen vehicle tracking devices, a similar pattern was found for likely similar reasons. Rural and urban departments serving populations less than 25,000 were more likely to cite cost as a limiting factor with respect to acquisition; larger departments were more likely to consider reliability and risk or liability as also being important. Interestingly, training requirements were not viewed as being as important by departments serving populations of more than 225,000. The largest departments (greater than 225,000) were also more likely to cite public opinion as being an important consideration.

State police departments cited cost as being an important limiting factor for the vehicle stopping/tracking devices. Reliability, training requirements, and risk or liability were also considered by these departments to likely limit future acquisition.

COUNTER-TERRORISM

Since the 1995 bombing of the Alfred P. Murrah Federal Building in Oklahoma City, the federal government has paid increased attention to the threat of terrorist acts within the United States. Although domestic terrorism has fortunately remained largely a potential, rather than realized, problem for law enforcement, gauging the degree of preparedness for such situations is of interest.

As the following table (Table 10) shows, counter-terrorism technology is generally not available to the majority (55–75 percent) of local police departments and only a small percentage of departments indicate that the technology is "not needed." (LETS, 28).

In addition to querying agencies on the array of counter-terrorism technology which they had available, the RAND Police Survey also asked about whether agencies had received federal funds, equip-

---

[11]Electrical/engine disruption technology for vehicle stopping is not yet available. We interpret the survey response to mean that many departments expect such technology, if and when available, to be expensive.

Table 10

Counter-Terrorism Technology Available to Local Departments

Technology	Not Needed/NA	Not Available	Obsolete	Old but Serviceable	Modern/ State of the Art
Explosives detection	8%	62%	0%	9%	17%
Bomb containment/ disablement	8%	58%	0%	9%	21%
Chemical agent detection	8%	68%	0%	7%	12%
Radioactive agent detection	8%	63%	6%	8%	10%
Blister/nerve agent protective clothing	11%	75%	1%	3%	6%
Electronic listening	8%	55%	4%	11%	18%
Long-range video monitoring	9%	66%	5%	5%	12%

SOURCE: LETS, 28. Numbers are statistically adjusted percent of local departments responding as indicated.

ment, or training for response to chemical, biological, or nuclear (CBRN) incidents since 1997. Of local police departments, 8 percent indicated that they had received federal help in counter-terrorism technology in the past three years. Not surprisingly, the fraction of departments reporting receiving that aid increased significantly with the population served. While only more than 6 percent of small urban (less than 25,000 population) and rural departments reported receiving aid, just over 33 percent of departments serving the largest cities indicated receiving it (LETS, 34). The perceived usefulness of the aid that was received was also somewhat dependent on the size of the police departments. Between 75 and 95 percent of most departments believed that the aid at least somewhat improved their organizational capabilities in the listed areas (LETS, 35).

In considering these results it is important to note that RAND did not survey fire departments or other agencies that may be better equipped than police. In addition, the reader should be aware that there are two aspects of response to terrorism incidents: crisis management and consequence management. The federal government exercises lead authority and responsibility in crisis management. Final authority to make decisions on scene regarding the causes of the incident, securing the scene perimeter, identifying and rendering weapons safe, and capturing terrorists rests with the FBI's On-Scene Commander. State and local agencies exercise lead authority to make decisions regarding the consequences of terrorism, including decisions regarding rescue and treatment of casualties and protective actions for the community (OES, 1998, pp. 3–4). Local agencies, such as police, coroner, medical, mental health, public works, and utilities may be assisted in consequence management by the Federal Emergency Management Agency (FEMA) (OES, 1998, p. 51).

It should also be noted that all police agencies, depending on their jurisdiction and whether it contains or abuts any particularly attractive terrorist targets, will not have the same needs (either in kind or in magnitude) for terrorism preparedness resources.[12] To guide acquisition by departments that believe they do need the technologies, the Office for State and Local Domestic Preparedness Support (OSLDPS) has published an authorized equipment purchase list, which includes the following categories of equipment: personal protective, chemical and biological detection, and communications.[13]

For those interested in more information on this topic than is provided by the RAND survey, in Fiscal Year (FY) 1999 the Department of Justice funded a national assessment of state and local agencies' equipment capability, readiness, and training needs for chemical, biological, radiological, nuclear, and conventional explosive responses (Mitchell, 1999). That study is expected to produce more comprehensive data than we are able to provide here.

---

[12]This represents another instance in the survey where it is clear that the number of departments selecting "technology not needed" is almost certainly unreasonably low. Based on reasonable probabilities for terrorist incidents, it is obvious that the needs of major urban police forces and isolated rural departments would not be comparable. As a result, the responses to this question likely represent an unwillingness by respondents to indicate they do not want something that has the potential to bring resources to their departments. It is therefore likely to be more appropriate to view these figures as primarily descriptive. For the sake of illustration, it is doubtful that providing nerve agent protective clothing to every law enforcement agency in the United States would have as beneficial an effect on public safety (or even terrorism preparedness) as many other possible uses of those resources.

[13]See http://www.ojp.usdoj.gov/osldps/lib_fy99cm_appd.htm or current web site.

Chapter Four

INVESTIGATION AND APPREHENSION

When a crime has been committed and police have responded to the scene, law enforcement activity transitions in focus from situation management toward the goal of successfully identifying individual perpetrators and bringing them to justice. In this process of evidence collection and suspect identification, technology has many roles to play in broadening the capability and increasing the effectiveness of investigators.

Major findings from the chapter include:

- Most local police departments (90 percent) reported that they lacked technology to detect or analyze cyberattacks. Even for departments in large urban areas (more than 225,000 population), three quarters of departments reported that they lacked these capabilities. Among state police organizations, two-thirds do not currently use or have access to these technologies.
- The tasks associated with police interaction with the court system apparently represent an important opportunity to integrate technology into law enforcement. Only 5–15 percent of local departments and 10–25 percent of state police indicated that they link or share computerized files of summonses or warrants with other agencies. Furthermore, only 5 percent of local police reported having a video or other systems that allowed them to file cases with prosecutors remotely.

CRIMINAL INVESTIGATION

Digital Crime Scene Photography

The technique of photography has been important to law enforcement since soon after its invention and commercialization. The ability to capture accurate photographic evidence at a crime scene serves purposes from advancing an ongoing investigation to presenting a completed case in a court of law. Recent advances in digital photography, by increasing the speed of the technique, decreasing the individual cost of photos, and making the photographic output readily sharable over electronic networks, has the potential to be even more useful to law enforcement. As a result, it is of interest how many departments have access to the technique. The RAND Law Enforcement Survey found 31 percent of local police departments have digital crime scene photographic systems, while 13 percent of state police report using them (LETS, 16b).[1]

Fingerprint Identification

The FBI's Automated Fingerprint Identification System (AFIS) allows police to rapidly check fingerprints against those in a national database to identify known criminals or a suspect whose prints are in the system. AFIS is one component of the Integrated Automated Fingerprint Identification System (IAFIS), which is described in the accompanying text box.

Sixty-two percent of respondents to the RAND Forensics Survey have exclusive use of an AFIS terminal and another 28 percent have shared access to the system. Most state police have either exclusive ownership of an AFIS system, shared ownership of one, or have an AFIS terminal with access to a remote AFIS site. Fewer local police have AFIS access. Among local police, a far higher percentage of larger departments than smaller ones have access to AFIS.

---

[1]For the LETS survey to local police, percentages have been statistically adjusted to represent the entire population. See Appendix A for a description of the adjustment methodology. For the LETS survey to state police and the FTS survey to crime labs, results are reported as unadjusted percentages.

In order to interface with automated fingerprint matching systems, fingerprints can be captured digitally or can be collected in the "traditional" ink-on-paper method and scanned into a computer. Because of the increase in speed and efficiency of digital capture, this method represents an improvement over traditional methods. The RAND Law Enforcement Survey found that 21 percent of local departments make widespread use of digital imaging for fingerprints, 9 percent make limited use of such technology, and 70 percent do not use it. The percentage of departments making widespread use of this technology increases with size of population served. One-third of state police reported widespread use of digitized fingerprints.

Among local departments, 2 percent expressed no need for future acquisition or use of digitized fingerprints. Sixty-five percent saw cost as a factor inhibiting acquisition of this technology emphasizing the barrier to replacing the current traditional methods—given the relative cost differentials—with a new technology. Thirteen percent saw training as a limiting factor. Training was even more of a factor for state police with 20 percent highlighting it as a potential barrier to acquisition. This suggests that there are potential technology adoption issues associated with this technology in addition to how its cost compares to current methods.

Although many parts of a police department may be involved in fingerprinting and print collection, crime labs perform much of the analysis of the evidence. The RAND Forensic Survey found that requests for latent print processing accounted for about 16 percent of all requests to crime labs. On average, labs reported processing 90 percent of requests received (FTS, 22).

Crime labs experiencing problems in obtaining latent print analysis in sufficient time to meet legal or other timeframe requirements were asked to indicate whether this was due to backlogs, lack of technology or equipment, prohibitive costs, and/or lack of trained personnel. Nearly all respondents said that backlogs were a reason for the problems. More than half cited lack of trained personnel, while 12 percent cited lack of technology or equipment. None of the respondents saw prohibitive cost as a reason for their problems with latent prints (FTS, 28a). This suggests that, for crime labs, the human factors (in this case lack of personnel in addition to their training) associated with the technology are by far the dominant influence on effective deployment of the techniques.

Suspect Composites

Just as is the case for photography, digital technology has the potential to improve the way law enforcement agencies generate and use composite sketches of crime suspects. The RAND survey found that 14 percent of local police departments make widespread use of digital imagery for suspect composites, 31 percent make limited use of it, and 55 percent do not use it. The percentage of departments making widespread use of this technology increases with size of population served. Two-thirds of state police reported limited use of suspect composites (LETS, 36g).

Among local departments, only 5 percent saw no need for future acquisition or use of digitized composite sketches. Forty-eight percent saw cost as a factor limiting acquisition or use of this technology. Twenty-one percent saw training and 11 percent effectiveness or reliability as limiting factors (LETS, 36g). This suggests that agencies have some concerns about how digital composites will be effectively integrated into their current operations.

Cybercrime

With the advent of the Internet, the connection of more and more computers to the common network, and the growth of e-commerce, cybercrime has become an increasing challenge for both the country as a whole and the law enforcement community. An ABC Television News report of February 28, 1998, estimated that U.S. corporations sustain damages in excess of $10 billion annually from cyberattacks (Sandia National Laboratories, 1998, p. 32). Thirty percent of respondents to a recent survey from both private and public sectors reported having been subjected to cyberattacks (Computer Security Institute, 1999). The Presidential Commission on Critical Infrastructure Protection concluded, "Federal R&D efforts are inadequate for the size of the R&D challenge presented by emerging cyber threats" and expressed their belief that "real-time detection, identification, and response tools are urgently needed" (President's Commission, 1997, p. 89).

Victims of cybercrime are often more concerned with repairing the damage and limiting further damage than in reporting it as a crime, and rely much less on law enforcement for assistance. The differences in how private entities respond to these crimes, in addition to the broad variety of cybercrimes that can be perpetrated, are increasingly problematic for law enforcement.[2] The need to attract human resources with the needed knowledge to respond to these crimes, coupled with the cost of the necessary computer technology, make it even more difficult and straining to already burdened organizations (Joint Report, 2000).

The LECTAC Law Enforcement Operations Subcommittee has identified cybercrime as a high priority concern (LECTAC, 2000, p. 39). The LECTAC Forensic and Investigative Sciences Subcommittee has called for a higher emphasis on methods and best practices for electronic evidence and electronic crime-monitoring in general (LECTAC, 2000, p. 37). Looking into the future, a British panel forecasting toward 2010 anticipates increasing difficulty for law enforcement from information and communications technology (ICT)–linked crime.

> The domination of, and changes brought about by, these technologies will have a profound effect upon crime. In particular the potential for its increased speed and scale. Crimes such as electronic theft and fraud will occur more quickly, reducing the likelihood of being caught in the act. Information about how to compromise a system will be available more quickly and to more people. As the lingua franca of the internet, sites or communication in English may disproportionately be targets for crime and disruption.
>
> As well as its speed and scale, ICTs offer greater complexity. This will be significant in terms of setting standards; international crime;

[2]A recent New Jersey study (Joint Report, 2000) addressed the following types of computer crime:

- Crimes against children,
- Bias and hate crimes,
- Hacking,
- Internet fraud,
- Identity theft,
- Internet gambling, and
- E-commerce in alcoholic beverages and tobacco.

> police jurisdictions; judicial systems; and legislation. The acceptability of digital evidence[3] in court—and the ability for it to be understood—are issues to consider. Potential solutions to crime need to be understood by those using them—complex or lengthy security procedures will most likely be ignored. ICTs will also allow the increasingly sophisticated use of cryptography and steganography[4] to conceal illegal transactions (Crime Prevention Panel, 2000, p. 4).

E-mail and the Internet promote asynchronous, global, collaborative communication,[5] which tends to flatten hierarchy and break down walls between organizations. This will create both new challenges and opportunities.

> To cope with info-crimes, the police and other authorities will need to adapt their techniques to the characteristics and tricks of the Information Marketplace, as they have begun to do. But the broad framework in which they perform these jobs can remain the same.

In order for law enforcement to adapt to these changes, changes are required far above the local level: Increased coordination of laws among different states and different nations will be critical for the simple reason that cyberspace does not recognize [state or] national boundaries (Dertouzos, 1997, p. 289). Currently, law enforcement at the state and local level is not prepared for these types of challenges, even without their international complications.

The RAND Law Enforcement Survey asked respondents to rate the quality or adequacy of technologies currently owned or available to their agency to detect and analyze cyberattacks. Ninety percent of local police departments indicated such technology was not currently in use or available to their agency; although a quarter of departments serving urban populations of more than 225,000 did indicate access to or usage of these technologies. Of these departments, 15 percent rated the technologies available to their agency as being modern/

---

[3]Material derived from a computer, electronic system, or presented in an electronic form.

[4]Steganography, the means by which images are hidden within others, can be used to send seemingly innocent images that contain illegal images or information.

[5]See Barksdale, p. 95 in Hesselbein et al. (1998).

state of the art (LETS, 28h). Among state police, two-thirds did not currently use or have available to their department technologies to detect and analyze cyberattacks. Of those that did, only two departments rated the technology as being modern/state of the art (LETS, 28h).

Given the apparent lack of availability of cybercrime resources in local departments, it was of interest whether these organizations were seeking assistance (and from where they were seeking it) to deal with this threat. When asked to identify where they had sought assistance, a full 73 percent of the police departments did not list *any* sources of help. Of those indicating that their department had sought assistance, the advice was overwhelmingly sought from in-house sources (Table 11). In addition it is noteworthy that such a small fraction of local departments have sought help in this area from any source. Although the implications of this result are somewhat ambiguous—since they could mean either that cybercrime is not occurring within the jurisdictions of most local departments or simply that the departments are not being called on to respond to it—it might imply that these departments should be better informed of the resources which are available to assist them in this area. These data are discussed in more detail in later chapters on federal support of state and local police organizations.

Table 11

Percent of State and Local Police Receiving Cybercrime Investigation or Analysis Support from Various Sources Within Past Year

	In-House	Local Agency	State Agency	Manu-facturer	NLECTC	FBI	ATF	Nat'l Labs	Other
Local police	24%	14%	14%	2%	1%	0%	0%	0%	0%
State police	53%	7%	20%	7%	0%	20%	0%	0%	7%

SOURCE: LETS, 32a. Numbers are percent of departments reporting they received technology-related support from indicated sources in the past year. Local departments are statistically adjusted percentages based on sample weighting.

SUSPECT APPREHENSION

Summonses and Warrants

Court-related functions—which include executing arrest warrants, providing court security, serving civil processes, and serving as witnesses—are all labor intensive. Because of their duties and responsibilities at the local level, most law enforcement organizations are involved in a number of court-related functions. Most local police execute arrest warrants. Additionally, nearly all sheriffs' departments provide court security and serve civil processes (Table 12).

Because of the labor-intensive nature of these processes, technology has a significant opportunity to positively affect their execution. Technology can increase the efficiency of court-related functions if files, such as those containing information on summonses and warrants, can be shared with other agencies. From the RAND survey results, it is clear that little has been done to integrate technology into the court process at the local level, regardless of size of department. Only 5–15 percent of local police actually share or link computerized files of summonses and warrants with other agencies. Those state police (about 10–25 percent) that do link with or share such files do so with either other state agencies or other agencies. Very few of these departments link or share files with nearby cities or with county agencies (LETS, 23i,m).

Table 12

Percent of Agencies with Primary Responsibility for Court-Related Functions, 1997

	County Police	Municipal Police	Sheriff	State Police
Execute arrest warrants	87%	93%	98%	55%
Provide court security	10%	22%	93%	8%
Serve civil process	17%	5%	93%	6%

SOURCE: Reaves and Goldberg, 1999, p. xvi. Data are for agencies with 100 or more officers. "State Police" are primary state police.

Mug Shots

Beyond the advantages of digital photography at crime scenes that were discussed above, this technology can also improve the efficiency of the mug shots taken when individuals are brought into custody. It appears that this digital technology is somewhat more widespread than that used in crime scene photography. The RAND survey found that 43 percent of local police departments make widespread use of digital imaging for mug shots, 19 percent make limited use of this technology, and 38 percent do not use it. The percentage of departments making widespread use of this technology also increases with size of population served.

In contrast to its adoption at the local level, only 13 percent of state police reported widespread use of digitized mug shots.

Among local departments, 6 percent expressed no need for future acquisition or use of digital mug shots. Forty-seven percent saw cost as a factor acquisition or use of this technology (LETS, 36f). Like the digital fingerprint case discussed above, this cost concern could represent as much satisfaction with currently used "lower tech" methods (which reduce the perceived benefit of changing) as the absolute costs of the systems themselves. This could be particularly important for departments that do not have to process a large volume of individuals taken into custody.

Remote Case Filing

Because of the travel and time that can be involved, the process of filing cases with prosecutors represents another key area in which technology could have a significant effect on law enforcement productivity and effectiveness. Information and communications technologies, in particular by allowing remote filing of cases, could potentially reduce workload and free up officers for other activities. From the results of the RAND Law Enforcement Technology Survey, it is clear that this particular technological capability is almost entirely absent from U.S. police forces. Only 5 percent of local police surveyed by RAND reported having a video or other system for remote case filing with prosecutors. None of the state police respondents reported having a remote case filing system (LETS, 16h).

Chapter Five

FORENSIC ANALYSIS

Forensic science is the application of scientific knowledge to legal problems or proceedings. In law enforcement, forensic science is largely concerned with testing physical and biological evidence to determine objective facts about what happened, when it happened, and who was involved. As a result, forensic science capability is important because it may yield information that is more accurate, precise, and reliable than eyewitness testimony or even confessions.[1] Such information, in turn, can increase the success of both investigations and trials in determining the facts of the case.

As the results of the RAND Forensic Technology Survey and accompanying case studies indicate, there is a pressing need for more and better forensic science technology—and for well-trained people to use it and present its results. Key findings include:

- Many crime laboratories have substantial backlogs of evidence not yet tested or otherwise processed. Clearing these backlogs is a major concern and goal of laboratory directors.
- In attempting to keep up with demand for forensic services, laboratories tend to support prosecutions better than they support investigations. The result is that fewer criminal investigations are aided than would be the case if more, timely forensic science ca-

[1]For compelling arguments supporting this, see Scheck, Neufeld, and Dwyer (2000).

pacity were available. This in turn would increase the likelihood of success.[2]

- Most laboratory directors face a constant struggle to obtain funding to replace and modernize laboratory equipment and to hire, train, and retain qualified staff. Many laboratories see a greater need for more staff and training to use technology than for more equipment itself.
- Recent court decisions are forcing forensic scientists to improve both the science upon which the technology is based and the competence of testifying examiners (i.e., expert witnesses in forensic science). Here, the issue is one of quality of the work product.
- Given the tight capability and staffing constraints under which forensic laboratories currently operate, research and development directed at providing technologies specifically aimed to increase lab throughput and staff efficiency could have a major positive impact. For example, successfully achieving the R&D goal of producing a forensic "appliance" that will reliably deliver a given analysis capability per unit time at reasonable cost with minimal human intervention could alleviate many of the pressures on the system.

TYPES OF CRIME

In an effort to gauge the capability and capacity of forensic science laboratories, the RAND Forensics Survey asked a number of questions about the labs' support of a number of types of investigations. In addition to the actual ability to perform analyses, when requests are part of ongoing investigation or prosecution, the time frame involved in which a laboratory does its job is also critical. As a result,

---

[2]Here is how one lab director described his situation to us: "While we are meeting most prosecution needs by trial date in all disciplines, we believe investigative support requires case turnaround in less than 30 days while the case is still active. This is especially true in property crimes, such as burglary, because the police case goes inactive. Slow turnaround limits the effectiveness of forensic databases such as AFIS. Police become discouraged from submitting evidence in cases without suspects or arrests. Low volume needs of investigators are not being met due to the high cost per sample of providing quality-assured service."

the survey asked the directors whether their labs generally performed none, some, most, or all of requested evidence tests within the time necessary for a number of different types of criminal investigations.[3]

Table 13 shows the percent of labs reporting they are likely to perform all or most tests, given that they had capability to perform at least some—that is, excluding those labs that do not handle the applicable test at all.

It should be noted that some of these numbers may be misleading, in that what the laboratories keep track of is whether they perform tests on evidence *submitted* to them. What we do not know is what percentage of evidence that could be collected and submitted actually is submitted for forensic analysis.

The survey asked respondents if availability of technology or trained personnel limited their laboratory's ability to analyze all evidence

Table 13

Percent of Labs Likely to Perform All or Most Tests, by Type of Crime

Crime	Print Analysis	Trace Analysis	DNA Analysis	Firearms Analysis
Murder	89%	73%	78%	86%
Assault	78%	53%	49%	79%
Rape	86%	64%	63%	78%
Hit & Run	83%	53%	50%	56%
Burglary	71%	44%	40%	73%
Auto Theft	76%	47%	46%	68%

SOURCE: FTS, 27. Values are percentages of those respondents (who had at least some capacity to perform each type of analysis) who indicated they were likely to perform all or most of the tests.

[3]It is important to note that the RAND Forensics Survey question on conductibility of analyses did not distinguish between meeting requirements for effective *investigation* and *prosecution.* Several respondents told us that they are much more likely to meet requirements for prosecution than for investigation. As one respondent put it, "We always meet court dates." As we discuss later in the report, we believe that limited forensic capacity shortchanges investigations—probably seriously—especially in cases where no suspect has yet been identified.

Table 14

Factors Limiting Analysis, by Type of Case

	Technology	Trained Personnel
Murder	26%	93%
Attempted Murder	25%	95%
Forcible Rape	23%	94%
DUI	31%	89%
Possession	17%	98%

SOURCE: FTS, 29. Numbers are percent of respondents selecting each factor as a barrier to analysis.

submitted in various types of cases (Table 14). Although technology is seen as a limiting factor by about a quarter of the laboratories, lack of trained personnel is seen as a factor by almost all of them. This is one of the major findings of the study.[4]

In light of this finding, it is clear that forensic laboratories face technological problems but, more seriously, human capital and human resource issues. It is also reasonable to assume that shortages of trained personnel will also magnify any organizational technology adoption problems; when the workload on employees is very high, they seldom have time to pursue the adoption of new technology. Although the most obvious approaches to these problems are human resource directed (including increasing staff, training, and salaries to boost retention), technology could also play a role as well. Technological advances that increase staff productivity, automate analyses, or streamline management could improve the situation by leveraging current human resources.

TYPES OF EVIDENCE

In examining the ways technology might be integrated into forensics laboratories to increase their efficiency and effectiveness, an understanding of the nature of their workload is essential. The RAND

[4]For the LETS survey to local police, percentages have been statistically adjusted to represent the entire population. See Appendix A for a description of the adjustment methodology. For the LETS survey to state police and the FTS survey to crime labs, results are reported as unadjusted percentages.

Forensics Survey found that for the most recent year each lab compiled data, more than half of the workload in terms of their primary unit of measurement was for tests of controlled substances, about a sixth was for latent prints, and a ninth for blood alcohol tests.[5] Percentages of each analysis, including the nine categories that make up the remainder of the workload, are included in Table 15.

Controlled Substances

Controlled substances are those drugs and drug products specified by the Controlled Substances Act (Title II of the Comprehensive Drug Abuse Prevention and Control Act of 1970). The explanation for the large fraction of controlled substance analysis in laboratory workload is thought to come from two basic reasons. First, due to the scope of the drug problem in America, there are many controlled substance cases; second, under current law, a controlled substance case con-

Table 15

Distribution of Evidence Received by Laboratories

Type of Evidence	Percent of Total Received[a]	Type of Evidence	Percent of Total Received
Controlled substances	53.57%	DNA	2.19%
Latent prints	15.70%	Trace analysis	1.59%
Blood alcohol	10.74%	Questioned documents	1.09%
Toxicology	6.88%	Fire debris	0.47%
Firearms, tool marks, etc.	4.51%	Computer crime evidence	0.07%
Forensic biology	3.19%	Explosive residue	0.03%

SOURCE: FTS, 22. Values are percentages for each analysis of the total number of all tests that responding laboratories reported.

[a]A few respondents included fire and explosive debris in trace evidence, and a few included blood alcohol in toxicology. A few labs reported number analyzed exceeding number received; this may reflect confirmation tests following screening tests.

[5]Most labs use the *case* as their primary unit of measurement of evidence received and analyzed; however, some measure their work in terms of submissions, work requests, or items of evidence.

viction requires analytical confirmation that the evidence is, in fact, a controlled substance. Since this one activity represents such a large fraction of laboratory workload, it is important to note that even small improvements in efficiency for these tests could have significant overall results. The RAND Forensics Survey found that requests for tests for controlled substances accounted for more than half of all submissions to crime labs. On average, labs reported analyzing evidence in 90 percent of requests received (FTS, 22).

Latent Prints

Fingerprint analysis, discussed previously in Chapter 4, represents the next most common test performed by the crime labs responding to the RAND survey. Latent print analysis accounts for approximately 16 percent of laboratory workload. On average, the labs reported processing 90 percent of the print analysis requests received (FTS, 22).

Toxicology and Blood Alcohol

The RAND Forensics Survey found that requests for tests for blood alcohol and toxicology accounted for about 11 percent and 7 percent, respectively, of all submissions to crime labs. On average, labs reported analyzing evidence in 97 percent of blood alcohol and 96 percent of toxicology requests received (FTS, 22).

Forensic Biology Screening

The RAND survey found that requests for forensic biology screening accounted for about 3 percent of all submissions to crime labs. On average, labs reported analyzing evidence in 96 percent of requests received (FTS, 22).

Computer Crime Evidence

The RAND survey found that requests for computer crime analysis accounted for only 0.07 percent of all requests to crime labs. On average, labs reported processing 78 percent of requests received (FTS, 22).[6]

Firearms, Tool Marks, Footwear, and Tire Prints

The RAND survey found that requests for firearms, tool mark, footwear, or tire print forensics accounted for about 5 percent of all requests to crime labs. On average, labs reported processing 83 percent of requests received.

Those respondents experiencing problems in processing firearms analysis in sufficient time to meet legal or other timeframe requirements were asked to indicate whether this was due to backlogs, lack of technology or equipment, prohibitive costs, and/or lack of trained personnel (Table 16). The respondents overwhelmingly cited backlogs and personnel shortage as the reasons.

In fact, firearms analysis represents a case where technology has already gone a long way to reduce reliance on slow, manual analysis. Until recently, microscopic comparison of shell casings and fired

Table 16

Reasons Cited for Problems in Conducting Firearms Analyses

Backlogs	79%
Technology/Equipment	10%
Costs Prohibitive	2%
Trained Personnel	69%

SOURCE: FTS, 28a. Numbers are percent of responses.

[6]Our surveys failed to distinguish between type of crime and type of evidence. Crimes labeled "cybercrime," "computer crime," or "electronic crime" include hacking or cracking, theft of electronic funds or identity, use of the Internet for illegal gambling or child pornography, denial of service attacks, etc. Types of evidence called "electronic evidence" or "digital evidence" include computers, hard disk drives, electronic mail, etc. Investigation and prosecution of electronic crime may or may not include analysis of digital evidence. Similarly, digital evidence may bear on electronic crime as well as other types of cases.

bullets was done manually by a firearms examiner. In the early 1990s, two automated computer-based systems were developed: the Bureau of Alcohol, Tobacco and Firearms (ATF) fielded its Integrated Ballistics Identification System (IBIS) and the Federal Bureau of Investigation (FBI) fielded its DrugFire system. Both systems, though not interoperable with one another, digitize impressions on shell casings or bullet fragments and rapidly compare the images with those in the systems' databases. Any matches that are identified can link investigations of separate crimes committed using the same firearms. In 1999, the ATF and FBI, working together through the National Integrated Ballistics Information Network (NIBIN) announced that:

> [The] two agencies would coordinate their efforts and merge the best of both systems, bringing to law enforcement the latest technology for ballistic examination.
>
> ATF will have overall responsibility for all system sites and the FBI will establish and maintain a secure high-speed communications network. The resulting single, unified system will form the backbone of a network eventually capable of identifying the individual fingerprint left by virtually every gun used in a violent crime.[7]

The vision behind this systems integration, which serves as an apt illustration of the optimism that technology will continue to revolutionize forensic investigation, is included in the following textbox.

Currently, 72 percent of respondents to the RAND survey have either exclusive or shared access to the FBI's DrugFire computerized technology to associate previously unrelated firearms involved in crimes. Twenty-three percent have access to IBIS (Integrated Ballistics Identification System). Only 10 percent of responding labs reported not having access to either system.[8,9]

---

[7]Tracy Hite, The National Integrated Ballistics Information Network, *The Police Chief*, April 2000, p. 2.

[8]Almost all of these are specialized labs that do not process firearms evidence.

[9]Over time, DrugFire will be phased out and replaced by the National Integrated Ballistics Identification System (NIBIS).

State Attorney Generals' Vision for Firearms Identification

We look forward to a day when at any gun crime scene in America, a van pulls up with the tracing equipment, cartridges found at the scene are scanned into the machine, the scanned image is checked against the joined computer databases of the FBI and the ATF, the "matches" are selected by the computer and forwarded electronically to a firearms examiner, and the firearms examiner selects the best match and wires the result, together with information about the matched weapon, back to the police at the scene of the crime. Ideally, this could all happen while the cartridges were still warm.[10]

Trace Evidence, Fire Debris, and Explosive Residue

Of the total requests to crime labs, the RAND survey found that requests for trace evidence, fire debris, and explosive residue tests accounted for about 4 percent, 1.5 percent, and 0.5 percent respectively. On average, labs reported performing analyses in 84 percent of cases where trace evidence was submitted, in 91 percent for fire debris cases, and 88 percent in explosive residue cases.

Those respondents experiencing problems in trace analysis in sufficient time to meet legal or other timeframe requirements were asked to indicate whether this was due to backlogs, lack of technology or equipment, prohibitive costs, and/or lack of trained personnel. The results for trace evidence analysis are included in Table 17.

It is noteworthy to point out that, in this area, analytical problems derive much more from technology issues than the problems with the other testing procedures discussed previously. Although backlogs and personnel are still the most important issues, more than 50 percent of lab directors cited technology as a source of concern.

[10]National Association of Attorneys General letter, June 12, 2000, posted at http://www.nibin.gov/documents/061200.naagletter.pdf.

Table 17

Reasons Cited for Problems in Conducting Trace Evidence Analyses

Backlogs	71%
Technology/Equipment	55%
Costs Prohibitive	14%
Trained Personnel	65%

SOURCE: FTS, 28a. Numbers are percent of responses.

Questioned Document Analysis

The RAND survey found that requests for questioned document analysis accounted for less than 1 percent of all requests to crime labs. On average, labs reported processing 93 percent of requests received.

TYPES OF EQUIPMENT

To help the non-specialist appreciate the range of technology required by a modern forensics laboratory, we quote a portion of an "appreciation of the situation" sent by a lab director along with his completed survey; footnotes have been added to define the technical terms.

> Crime laboratories apply technological advancements in science and engineering to solve forensic problems. For us, technology mainly means analytical instrumentation. If we had the money we would be considering a Raman spectrometer[11] for drug and trace analysis, or an ICP-MS[12] for glass or GSR[13] examinations. The last

[11]Raman spectrometer: an instrument for detailed spectral analysis of aqueous solutions, gels, powders, coatings, and surface media. Prices start at $10,000.

[12]ICP-MS: Inductively Coupled Plasma—Mass Spectrometry, a versatile, rapid, and precise analytical technique that provides high-quality multi-element and isotopic analysis.

[13]GSR: gunshot residue. For photographs and more information, see http://www.mdpd.com/analphot.html#gunshot.

20 years have seen great advances in computerization of chemical analysis methods. Computer applications have special forensic potential in two distinct areas: automation and digital imaging.

We have an automated but antiquated SEM-EDX-GSR[14] analysis system. We have begun to investigate robotic sample preparation of toxicological samples for solid phase extraction and ELISA analysis.[15] If we had an automatic fiber finder for tape lifts, we would be able to pay more attention to fiber evidence.

We have a Grim2 unit[16] for determining refractive index of glass and Drugfire for cartridge cases, as well as a video camera on our trace comparison microscope. We have an obsolete DOYA infrared viewing system for questioned documents that we would like to replace with a VSC2000 digital imaging system.[17]

Training remains a vitally important issue. The ATF, DEA, and FBI laboratories have presented some of the most effective training for our analysts. Continuing education in both the theory and operation of instrumentation is necessary. Some of the areas that require bolstering in my own lab are:

- Computer skills.
- Results interpretation and statistics.
- Composition and formulation of manufactured products.
- Quality program management.

While funding is needed for modern analytical instrumentation, equally, if not more important, is each forensic scientist's professional development. Administrators should not squander funds on

---

[14]SEM: scanning electron microscopy. EDX: energy dispersive X-ray analysis.

[15]ELISA: Enzyme-Linked Immunosorbent Assay—A binding assay used to detect illegal drugs among other things.

[16]GRIM2 is an abbreviation for Glass Refractive Index Measurement, a very discriminating, non-destructive, technique used for glass comparison. For photographs and more information, see http://www.mdpd.com/analphot.html#glass.

[17]VSC2000 is a document examination workstation used to examine questioned documents in the near infrared regions of the spectrum, through microspectrometry, color imaging, color coordinate measurement, image archiving, and casework management.

> fancy hardware left to sit blinking in the corner because the analysts know only how to push the 'ON' button.

In addition to characterizing the complexity of the demands placed on these labs and the requirements necessary to meet them, such a case study also emphasizes that technology adoption is important in addition to technology acquisition—so "fancy hardware [isn't] left to sit blinking in the corner."

General Lab Equipment

Though it was not feasible to ask for assessments of the quality or adequacy of all technology or equipment used in crime labs, the RAND Forensics Survey asked respondents to rate the quality of five types of equipment an earlier study of labs in California (California State Auditor, 1998) had found lacking. These are: computers, FTIRs,[18] GC[19] instruments, GC/MS[20] instruments, and microscopes (Table 18).

Overall, a large fraction of the respondents reported that their laboratory equipment is either "modern" or "state of the art" suggesting that, at least for these specific instruments, many crime labs are reasonably well outfitted. The slightly larger number of aging GC

Table 18

Quality of Laboratory Technologies in Use

	Obsolete	Old but Serviceable	Modern	State of the Art
Computers	3%	27%	56%	15%
FTIRs	1%	33%	41%	25%
GC Inst	1%	41%	37%	21%
GC/MS	1%	17%	48%	33%
Microscopes	6%	44%	33%	17%

SOURCE: FTS, 26. Numbers are percent of respondents.

[18]FTIRs: Fourier Transform Infrared Spectrometers.

[19]GC: Gas Chromatograph.

[20]GC/MS: Gas Chromatograph/Mass Spectrometer.

instruments is understandable given that, for many functions, a GC/MS is a superior instrument to a GC alone; labs may therefore not move to replace an aging GC rapidly, if at all. It should be noted that if the "old but serviceable" category on this survey is considered equivalent to the judgment that a piece of equipment is "outdated" in the previously cited California survey (California State Auditor, 1998), then the results from the two studies are roughly comparable.

Laboratory Information Management (LIM) Systems

Because of the complexity and variety of the tasks forensic laboratories are called on to perform, management of the submitted evidence and resulting workflow is a potential stumbling block. Such management tasks can be greatly facilitated by technology. In this area, a significant amount of technology has already been integrated into the nation's laboratories. Fifty-five percent of respondents to the RAND survey have fully computerized, networked management information systems; more than a third of the others have partially computerized systems (FTS, 30).

DNA Analysis

With the power of DNA analysis to contribute to criminal investigation gradually becoming more and more clear, the requirements on forensics laboratories to perform these tests are only likely to increase from the relatively modest fraction (approximately 2.2 percent) of current workload (FTS, 22). Even at the current rate of utilization, the demand for testing is exceeding current capability. In 1997 and again in 2000, the Bureau of Justice Statistics (BJS) fielded national surveys of DNA laboratories. The 1997 survey results, published in 2000, noted that 69 percent of publicly operated forensic crime labs across the nation reported a DNA analyses backlog of 6,800 known and unknown subject cases and 297,000 convicted offender samples. To alleviate case backlogs, 44 percent of the labs had hired additional staff, and 13 percent were contracting with private labs (Steadman, 2000, p. 1).

This increase in backlog is also being fueled by a change in the analysis procedure:

> Presently, the change from the time consuming Restriction Fragment Length Polymorphism (RFLP) technology to the Polymerase Chain Reaction (PCR) based Short Tandem Repeat (STR) technology, which is now being used in the national DNA database, requires that each offender sample and all casework samples be reanalyzed using STR technology. This is a tremendous task which requires enormous resources. Additionally, the national DNA database will not successfully work if the casework, particularly *no-suspect* casework, is not analyzed and entered into the database. ... When one looks at this *no-suspect* casework on a national level, the challenges are staggering (Sheppo, 2000, p. 2).

Although the change to a more straightforward test can be beneficial over the long term, it can have short-term consequences in increased workload. In addition, the desire to leverage the power of a database system to help solve current "no-suspect" cases requires that many more tests, on samples that may have no short-term "payoff," must be done.

In addition to the demand for testing stretching laboratory capacity, the long-term sample storage requirements associated with the use of DNA evidence is also becoming a concern:

> Most labs store samples of DNA in case there is a need to reanalyze the DNA evidence in the future. The most common forms in which labs stored DNA for retesting were extracted DNA, used by 88% of labs that stored DNA, and cuttings and swabs stored by 82% of those labs. ...Eighty-six percent of labs that stored DNA stored it frozen, and 22% stored it ultra-frozen.
>
> The labs' capabilities to store DNA ranged from 500 to 250,000 samples. On average 52% of their storage capacity was being used. Of DNA labs that saved DNA samples, about 80% stored the samples indefinitely, and the remaining labs reported storing DNA samples from 2 to 84 months. The median time DNA samples were stored by those labs was 24 months (Steadman, 2000, p. 9).

Lack of storage for evidence is becoming a problem of increasing concern. Public Law No. 106-546, the DNA Analysis Backlog Elimination Act of 2000, includes a provision that "Congress should condition forensic science-related grants to a State or State forensic facility on the State's agreement to ensure post-conviction DNA testing in appropriate cases." Ensuring post-conviction testing requires storing evidence indefinitely. The Deputy Attorney General of California, acknowledging the difficulty in making cost projections, estimated evidence storage costs for California at "$7.2 million to build new facilities, with yearly energy costs of about $1.2 million to sustain the facilities plus the cost of leasing space."[21]

At the laboratory level, approximately three-quarters of DNA lab budgets are devoted to personnel costs and supplies (Steadman, 2000, p. 5); any funding of equipment must come out of the remainder.[22] The level of equipment available at forensic labs was one topic of the 1997 BJS survey (mentioned above). The 108 publicly funded forensic laboratories responding to the survey reported owning a total of 292 thermocyclers[23] and 183 automated DNA analyzers. The HLA DQ Alpha test was used by 73 of the forensic labs for casework analysis, while 67 labs used the Polymarker kit and 41 labs tested for D1S80. (It should be noted that laboratories may use more than one type of assay.) At the time of that survey, 44 crime labs were examining short tandem repeats (STRs) using Profiler Plus, a commercially available STR kit. For analysis of convicted offender samples, 17 labs used Profiler Plus and 13 labs used Cofiler.[24] While 30 laboratories reported that they planned to use robotics for forensic DNA analysis, only six labs reported current use in one or more of the

---

[21]Statement of Enid A. Camps, June 13, 2000, http://www.senate.gov/~judiciary/6132000_eac.htm.

[22]One DNA lab director responding to the RAND survey described his staffing problem as follows: "The biggest problem facing our DNA laboratory is the lack of fully trained staff. Because almost every crime laboratory in the country is expanding its DNA programs, analysts with DNA experience are in high demand. Since our laboratory is also increasing its staffing levels, we are attempting to hire experienced staff but are unable to do so because of our relatively low salaries. Therefore, we must rely on our experienced staff to train the newly hired staff and, by doing so, we decrease our case output. To make matters worse, once the newly hired staff are trained, they resign and take higher paying positions."

[23]A thermocycler is an instrument used for performing the polymerase chain reaction (PCR). PCR takes very small amounts of DNA from biological evidence and produces millions of copies. This process results in sufficient DNA to allow the laboratory to generate a DNA profile from very small amounts of starting material.

[24]HLA DQ Alpha, Polymarker, and D1S80 were the first PCR-based tests used to examine biological forensic evidence. Additional PCR-based assays were later developed for detection of short tandem repeats (STRs). STRs are present in several locations throughout the DNA, and examining a series of STRs results in a higher level of discrimination than was achievable with the earlier PCR-based tests. Profiler Plus and Cofiler are two commercially available kits for STR analysis.

steps in the DNA analysis process. Four of the six labs used robotics for DNA spotting or aliquoting, five used robotics for DNA extraction, two labs used robotics for PCR reaction set up, and five used robotics in the DNA separation and analysis step.

Since the time of the BJS survey in 1997, many more public laboratories have implemented STR analysis for forensic casework. As the National Commission on the Future of DNA Evidence noted in 1999:[25]

> In the near future, DNA testing at a number of STR locations will likely replace RFLP and earlier PCR-based tests in most laboratories throughout the United States and the world. The Federal Bureau of Investigation (FBI) has recently established the 13 core STR sequences that will be used in the Combined DNA Index System (CODIS) database of convicted offenders.

In the same report, the Commission also noted the potential of mitochondrial DNA for forensic analysis:

> Mitochondrial DNA testing is generally performed on samples that are unsuitable for RFLP or PCR testing of nuclear DNA, such as dried bones or teeth, hair shafts, or any other samples that contain very little or highly degraded nuclear DNA. Mitochondrial DNA testing of forensic samples is increasing in the United States and throughout the world; at this time testing is available only in a limited number of laboratories.

The RAND Forensics Technology Survey addressed both the current and future use of DNA analysis in the contacted labs. In aggregate, 65 percent of respondents to the RAND survey have capability to perform DNA analysis. Of these, 92 percent have the ability to analyze DNA in ways that are compatible and integrated with the FBI's Combined DNA Index System (CODIS).[26]

---

[25] *Postconviction DNA Testing: Recommendations for Handling Requests* (1999). A Report from the National Commission on the Future of DNA Evidence, p. 28

[26] The 1994 Crime Act established the Combined DNA Index System (CODIS), a national DNA database program (http://www.ojp.usdoj.gov/bjs/pub/ascii/bjsfy98.txt) similar to AFIS, enabling State and local law enforcement crime laboratories to exchange and compare DNA information electronically. All 50 states and the District of Columbia have passed legislation requiring collection of DNA samples, primarily

The RAND survey found that requests for DNA tests accounted for only 2.19 percent of all submissions to crime labs. On average, labs reported analyzing evidence in 80 percent of requests received. This was the lowest rate for any type test queried in the survey, except for computer crime analysis, which had a slightly lower rate.

Respondents were also asked to indicate current use and any factors limiting future use of three specific DNA analysis methodologies: Short Tandem Repeats (STRs), Restriction Fragment Length Polymorphisms (RFLP), and Mitochondrial DNA tests. Current use of these techniques, as reported by survey respondents, is dramatically weighted toward the STR test; that particular analysis is in widespread use by 79 percent of labs and limited use by another 11 percent. The RFLP test is performed by only 14 percent of labs (with only 2 percent indicating widespread use). Testing of mitochondrial DNA is performed by only 4 percent of laboratories (FTS, 25).

The survey also asked what factors are seen as limiting future acquisition or use of the alternative DNA technologies.

The widespread perception on the part of respondents that RFLP analysis is unnecessary would logically reflect the replacement of this test by the simpler STR procedure (see Table 19). This case also represents the clearest example in these surveys of an instance where the respondents unambiguously issued a judgment "against" a technology. It is also clear that the consensus of respondents is that the STR test is necessary; of those identifying roadblocks to its use, it is noteworthy that trained personnel and laboratory space outweigh cost as the primary obstacles. For the mitochondrial DNA testing, a significant fraction of the respondents sees no need for the technol-

---

from sex offenders and other violent criminals. The FBI provides CODIS software, installation, training, and user support free of charge to any state or local law enforcement lab performing DNA analysis (Steadman, 2000, p. 10).

The State Identification Systems (SIS) Program is administered by BJA with funding from the FBI, to enhance capability of state and local governments to identity and prosecute offenders by establishing or upgrading information systems and DNA analysis capabilities. One purpose is to improve the ability to analyze DNA in ways that are compatible and integrated with CODIS (Steadman, 2000, p. 3).

Table 19

Factors Limiting Future Acquisition/Use of DNA Methodology

	No Need	Cost	Effectiveness/ Reliability	Training	Trained Personnel	Equipment or Lab Space
STR	2%	30%	2%	11%	57%	45%
RFLP	52%	10%	5%	5%	7%	7%
Mitochondrial	21%	51%	7%	42%	53%	56%

SOURCE: FTS, 25. Values are percentages of respondents who indicated each barrier to acquisition.

ogy, likely reflecting its more specialized nature. Of those that did see a need for it, indicated high barriers in all areas with the single exception of confidence in the technology itself (FTS, 25).

Those respondents experiencing problems in conducting DNA analysis in sufficient time to meet legal or other timeframe requirements were asked to indicate whether this was due to backlogs, lack of technology or equipment, prohibitive costs, and/or lack of trained personnel.

Although equipment and costs are seen as restricting ability of labs to perform all requested DNA analyses, backlogs and lack of trained personnel were far more frequently cited as causes for problems Table 20).

Table 20

Reasons Cited for Problems in Conducting DNA Analyses

Backlogs	84%
Technology/Equipment	24%
Costs Prohibitive	31%
Trained Personnel	76%

SOURCE: FTS, 28a. Numbers are percent of responses.

OVERALL STATED PRIORITIES

Interviews with laboratory directors conducted in the early stages of the study identified several candidate technology issues relevant to a broad range of crime labs. Survey respondents were then asked to evaluate these needs—including computerized evidence tracking, additional professional staff, training on available technology, additional laboratory space, continuing education and training, and overall laboratory management systems—and assign them high, medium or low priority (Table 21).

Although the survey respondents ranked laboratory management systems and evidence tracking the lowest priority, approximately one-third of the lab directors still ranked them as high priorities. At the other end of the spectrum, additional staffing and laboratory space were ranked as high priorities by a very large fraction of the respondents. Furthermore, it is noteworthy that continuing education on new technology and new developments in the field, in addition to receiving high priority rankings by two-thirds of the laboratory directors, was not ranked as low priority by *any* of the survey respondents.

It has been observed that the staffing situation at these laboratories (rated as a medium or high priority by more than 95 percent of respondents) may grow worse in the short term as the large cohort of experienced testifying examiners initially hired when the Law

Table 21

Stated Priorities of Laboratory Needs

Current Needs	Low	Medium	High
System for overall laboratory management	41%	28%	31%
Computerized system for tracking evidence	36%	27%	37%
Additional professional staffing	4%	17%	79%
Additional laboratory space	17%	17%	67%
Continuing education/in-service training on new technologies or new developments in the field	0%	33%	67%
Training on technology available or being acquired	3%	41%	56%

SOURCE: FTS, 15. Data depicted are percent of respondents.

Enforcement Assistance Administration (LEAA) was heavily supporting forensic science reaches retirement age.

Additional laboratory bench space was listed as a medium-to-high priority by almost 85 percent of respondents. The lack of sufficient laboratory space has required some laboratories have staff working different shifts share the same workspace and equipment. For calibration, survey respondents reported an average of 703 square feet of laboratory floor space per full-time staff member.

Clearing Backlogs

Although the demand for forensic science clearly testifies to the perceived value of the services, when resources are insufficient to deliver timely and accurate data to investigators and prosecutors, the efficiency of the system as a whole suffers.

> Each day forensic scientists are faced with the challenges of being absolutely accurate. In many cases, it is their conclusions that hold the keys to freedom or incarceration for the accused. While advancements in DNA, ballistics testing, and automated fingerprinting provide scientists with precision accuracy, backlogs have a chokehold on the United States Justice System (Milton E. Nix, Jr., Director, Georgia Bureau of Investigation).[27]
>
> While the use of quality forensic science services is widely accepted as a key to effective crime fighting, there currently exists in the United States a crisis ... caused by a shortage of forensic science resources. The criminal justice system relies heavily upon forensic

---

[27]Quoted in States' Coalition, *Crime Laboratory Crisis,* undated information package. This source identifies the following problems caused by backlogs in crime laboratories:

- Cases involving illegal drugs and drivers under the influence of alcohol or drugs (DUI) cannot move forward quickly, delaying timely prosecution.
- The results of DNA testing necessary where violent offenders are involved are backlogged, causing delays in the freeing of suspects or prosecution.
- The delay in processing toxicology tests is hindering benefactors from settling insurance claims and estates of loved ones that have died. Without toxicology reports, coroners cannot issue death certificates required by insurance companies.

For more information, contact Gale Bruckner, States' Coalition Director of Legislative and Intergovernmental Affairs at (404) 244-2501.

> science services as an integral part of the investigative and judicial process; however, these services have been long neglected. While billions of federal dollars have been spent on virtually every other criminal justice component—police officers, the courts, prisons, and information technology—the highly technical and expensive forensic sciences have received very little federal support. In most states and municipalities, funding has simply not kept pace with the increasing demand for crime laboratory analyses. This neglect has resulted in severe backlogs in forensic laboratories nationwide (Sheppo, 2000, pp. 2–3).

Backlogs are such a problem for so many forensic scientists that their vision does not extend beyond clearing the backlogs. Though local criminal justice systems would benefit from having integrated data and management systems for coordinating the work of police, laboratories, and courts, many jurisdictions struggling under the pressure of backlogs don't have the luxury of investing in such systems, though they would, in the long run, probably pay for themselves.

A survey conducted by *USA Today* in 1996 asked lab directors how they deal in the short run with their mushrooming caseloads with limited budgets and staff. Coping strategies included:

- **Prioritizing Cases**. Commonly, "the most serious cases and cases with set court dates are worked first. Some labs ... do minimal work on cases without a suspect, all but abdicating their crime-solving role."[28]
- **Random Sampling**. "This is a widely accepted approach in which labs test only a portion of confiscated drugs. But many labs don't

[28]Scheck, Neufeld, and Dwyer, in their book *Actual Innocence* (2000), have highlighted a number of ways technology could contribute to a more just law enforcement system. These include rapid use of DNA testing to minimize the incarceration of innocent suspects, application of DNA tests to evidence in unsolved crimes, and use of recording technology to provide an "objective record'"of witness identifications in line-ups and the results of police interrogation. They caution, however, that in order to be beneficial, forensic science must be objective. They advocate the need for budget independence from the police, the establishment of strong post-graduate programs in forensic science, and a hard-nosed examination of the techniques of the field to ensure that bad science is excluded from the courtroom. Independence of crime lab budgets was advocated by one laboratory director in the survey and a number of interviewees advocated the formation of post-graduate programs. We do not know how broadly either of these views are held within the forensic science community.

encourage random sampling and some jurisdictions, such as New York State, prohibit it, forcing technicians to spend countless extra hours doing analyses."

- **Training Police**. "Many labs don't have enough technicians to visit crime scenes and gather evidence, so they've begun training police to gather evidence and, in some cases, conduct a 'field test' of the evidence."
- **Automation**. "Some time-consuming tasks, such as analyzing multiple drug samples from a single, massive seizure, can be done automatically and, in many cases, during off hours."[29]
- **Charging Fees**. Some labs operate on a fee-for-service basis (*USA Today*, 1996).

Further research and exploration into strategies for dealing with increasing workload could provide transferable techniques that might be broadly applicable. While some analyses are amenable to automation at reasonable costs, others are not. Devising ways to automate additional tests could be an effective way to help labs increase efficiency. Furthermore, solid research into techniques (like random sampling of drug seizures discussed in the above list) could take the technique from a "non-encouraged coping strategy" to an established and validated technique.

Examples do exist of the power of both technology and organizational innovation to improve performance and effectiveness. In 1996 the Broward County Sheriff's Office crime lab in Fort Lauderdale had a backlog of less than 1 percent of the overall caseload, analyzing evidence from low priority property crimes and cases in which no suspect has been identified. Their crime lab examiners averaged

[29]"For example, a gas chromatograph/mass spectrometer, used to analyze drug samples, costs about $70,000. For another $10,000 or so, the machine can be purchased with an auto-sampler. That way, dozens of samples can be loaded into the machine at the end of the day and it will analyze them all overnight, saving time and freeing equipment time during working hours" (*USA Today*, 1996).

handling 1,200 cases annually, compared to the national average of 731. Time spent by crime lab examiners meeting with police and prosecutors was said to save "hundreds of analytical hours." Criminal courts and the lab are in the same building, saving lab examiners time they would otherwise have to spend traveling when they have to testify. Efforts are made to eliminate waste; for example, the lab ceased doing "conventional ABO blood typing analysis in favor of the much more accurate DNA analysis" (*USA Today*, 1996).

Trends Impacting Forensic Sciences

The growing range of techniques available to forensic sciences has clearly broadened the contribution they can make to law enforcement and criminal justice. Conversely, the increased number and technical requirements have contributed to the laboratories burgeoning workload. This has prompted a past president of the American Society of Crime Laboratory Directors to caution:

> Many forensic science professionals are concerned that the growing demands on laboratories have, or can have, a negative impact on the level of quality of the results achieved (Sheppo, 2000, p. 3).

Beyond concerns of pressure reducing quality, the expansion of new techniques also generate new and increasing demands on the knowledge base of laboratory employees. To help their employees master new technology, respondents to the Forensics Survey reported budgeting an average of $1,102 annually for training per testifying examiner. Given the high priority assigned to continuing education and technology training to keep up with technical advance, such an amount seems relatively low.

Support of Criminal Investigation and Prosecution

Demand for forensic analysis has been increasing and is expected to continue to increase. This stems from several factors, among them:

- Growth in numbers of police officers increases demand for forensic analysis of evidence to support criminal investigations.

- Increased awareness of types, capabilities, and limitations of forensic tests by prosecutors and defense attorneys, which began with the nationally televised O.J. Simpson murder trial, has increased demand for more extensive forensics analyses and testimony at trials.
- More rigorous standards for presentation of forensic evidence at trials, prompted by the Daubert[30] and other decisions, has increased demand for more careful and well-documented evidence of custody and laboratory procedure audits.

While all these trends can be positive ones from the perspective of overall functioning of the legal system and the contribution of forensic science to criminal justice, they only become so if they are supported by an adequate forensic science infrastructure.

Standards of Evidence

In the Daubert case, the Supreme Court established the Federal Rules of Evidence as superseding the Frye "general acceptance" test for admissibility of scientific evidence. In part, this requires that trial judges ensure that any and all scientific testimony or evidence admitted is not only relevant but also reliable. Additionally, in the case of a particular scientific technique, the court ordinarily should consider the known or potential rate of error and the existence and maintenance of standards controlling the technique's operation. Certain forensic science claims, such as "no two people have identical fingerprints," while passing the "general acceptance" test do not necessarily pass the Daubert test. This creates the need for more and better science undergirding "forensic science."

---

[30] 509 U.S. 579, 113 S.Ct. 2786, William DAUBERT, et ux., etc., et al., Petitioners, v MERRELL DOW PHARMACEUTICALS, INC No. 92-102 Supreme Court of the United States. Argued March 30, 1993. Decided June 28, 1993.

Recent Court Decisions Affecting Expert Testimony

Kumho Tire caps a trilogy that began in 1993 with *Daubert*, which held that the trial court judge was to serve as a gatekeeper under the Rules of Evidence to ensure the scientific validity of the expert's testimony. Four years later the Court fortified the gatekeeper role in *Joiner*, which held that appellate review of admissibility decision proceeds under an abuse of discretion standard. *Daubert* and *Joiner* together grant the trial court great power and leeway in admissibility decisions regarding expert witnesses: *Daubert* requires a judge to scrutinize expert testimony for scientific validity, *Joiner* protects the judge's decision from appellate review. *Kumho Tire* augments this discretion in two ways. First, *Kumho Tire* holds that the gatekeeping function applies to all expert testimony, not just testimony about a novel theory. Whether that of a physicist, clinical pathologist, epidemiologist, economist, sociologist, fireman, astronomer, computer programmer, or tire expert (at issue in *Kumho Tire*), the expert's testimony is subject to the trial judge's scrutiny for validity and reliability. The court also held that the standard the trial judge uses to determine validity was wide open and also subject to review under the abuse of discretion standard. Under *Kumho Tire*, not only is the trial court relatively free to exclude expert testimony, but also free to fashion the standard it uses for exclusion.[31]

BROADER VISIONS FOR FORENSIC SCIENCE TECHNOLOGY

Kevin Lothridge of the Consortium of Forensic Science Organizations (CFSO) has identified the following four main "drivers" for forensic science from the perspective of forensic science technology development:

- Realization of the power of DNA typing;
- Making best use of the availability of information data bases in latent print, firearms, and DNA;

[31]Shubha Ghosh, "Comment on *Kumho Tire*," http://www.law.umich.edu/thayer/ghokumho.htm. See also Margaret A. Berger, "Expert Testimony: The Supreme Court's Rules," at http://www.nap.edu.issues/16.4/berger.htm.

- Dealing with a demand for services that is close to crisis level; and
- Transitioning from a labor-intensive, craft-based activity to a highly technical and automated one (Lothridge, 2000).

If these drivers do indeed push technology development appropriately, Lothridge sees a very different vision of forensic science:

> As technology advances, the way crime scene and forensic investigations are conducted will change dramatically over the coming decade. There will be a move away from craft-based services. The focus of technology will be on-the-spot field-testing rather than batch testing in the laboratory. What batch testing that continues will be increasingly automated. The utility of testing will be enhanced by linkage to on-line databases. The lab-in-a-box concept will extend what has already happened with breath alcohol testing to other areas such as latent print development and comparison, body fluid typing, and drug analysis. Trained police personnel will conduct tests. The role of the crime laboratory will be conducting those tests not able to be converted to field use, plus managing and interpreting the test data, to reconstruct the sequence of events of the crime and present findings in court. The real vision for all the evidence collected at the crime scene is that the necessary items will have the appropriate forensic analysis performed within 24 hours (Lothridge, 2000).

There are, however, significant obstacles to the realization of this vision. Important roadblocks exist in technology development, the successful transfer of the technologies to law enforcement departments, understanding the implications of recent court rulings vis-à-vis testing performed by non-scientists, and being able to shift attention toward the future from dealing with today's problems (Lothridge, 2000). Some of these same issues and concerns are echoed in the responses to the RAND survey.

Possible areas of advancement in the intermediate term include integration of computational capabilities with biological, chemical, and optical components via a "systems-on-a-chip" approach. Already, such devices have been developed for basic DNA analysis. Related to the lab-on-a-chip concept is that of the more complete lab-in-a-box. At one time, alcohol intoxication testing was the sole province of laboratory technicians; now that testing has moved out into the field, as technology for field sobriety tests became available to police. In an analogous fashion, the idea of a lab-in-a-box does not necessarily demand any new tests or types of forensic analysis, rather it requires development and engineering to produce an appliance which, reliably and with as little human intervention as possible, generates a promised throughput of a set of routine analyses at a reasonable cost. If such appliances are portable, these advances in technology might make it possible to expand forensic science capacity markedly as police become equipped to do more evidence collecting and testing at the crime scene rather than in the lab.

The potential exists for significant improvements in the way forensic science is performed within the walls of the laboratory as well. The growing fields of microelectronic sensors and microelectromechanical systems (MEMS) may enable technologies that vastly improve automated test equipment or laboratory robotics and generate futuristic equipment such as robotic crime scene investigators. Many desirable databases—such as paint,[32] paper, and ink—currently do not exist or are not widely available. There is potential for teleforensics to help officers on the crime scene. Special lighting is demonstrating its usefulness for disclosing otherwise overlooked evidence. What these technology trends may mean for local crime labs is not clear. The potential exists that in this field, as it has in many other fields of science, equipment will become expensive and specialized enough that single labs can neither support nor fully utilize the "top of the line" instruments. If such a shift does occur, models such as investing in high-end, expensive equipment on a regional basis may have to be explored.

---

[32]Currently, more than 50 forensic laboratories are participating in development of the Paint Data Query (PDQ) database, used to identify the source of unknown automotive paint.

Chapter Six

ADMINISTRATION AND MANAGEMENT

Although the term "law enforcement technology" most readily evokes images of smart guns or DNA analysis, there are many "less glamorous" roles that can be played by technology that nonetheless can have a dramatic impact on the ability of law enforcement organizations to police their jurisdictions and ensure public safety. One of the main areas is the administration and management of departments and their deployment of their human and technical assets.

Some central findings of this chapter include:

- *Information Technology*—while most police officers now have access to computer technology in their workspaces, IT-related needs are still high priority for most departments. The existence of a "digital divide" between rural/small departments and large departments is troubling from the perspective of local law enforcement.
- *Training*—issues surrounding training, including both training on technology and technology to facilitate training, are clearly important. Departments reported significant shortfalls in training technology and raised questions about the quality of that which is available. More than half of local departments rated better technology to train their personnel as a high priority.
- *Technology Acquisition*—departments differ in their perceptions of the different risks associated with technology acquisition. In addition, perceived liability, technology reliability/effectiveness, and public opinion risks vary among different technologies. While state police organizations appear to ascribe a higher prior-

ity to information to aid technology acquisition, the great majority of all departments rate it as at least a medium priority.

- *Accountability*—while not as high a priority as some other concerns, technology to improve police accountability was listed as a high priority by a large fraction of departments. Not unexpectedly, this area is a higher priority for departments serving larger numbers of citizens.

INFORMATION PROCESSING

In a society constantly reminded of the potential of the Internet, it is almost unnecessary to point out the potential for information technologies to benefit the operations of an organization. In the case of law enforcement, where problems often involve the effective allocation of limited officers across an entire jurisdiction, complete, reliable, and timely information can be a "force multiplier," enabling law enforcement agencies to focus their resources more effectively.

Computer Hardware

According to the results of recent law enforcement surveys, most police departments have access to computers. The 1997 Law Enforcement Management and Administrative Statistics (LEMAS) study[1] found 82 percent of local police departments using workspace or centralized computers (Reaves and Goldberg, 2000, p. 24).

The RAND Law Enforcement Survey, conducted in 2000, found 96 percent of local police had computers in their workspaces.[2] Fifty-four percent of respondents to the RAND survey characterized their

---

[1]The findings of the LEMAS study were published as three reports: Reaves and Goldberg, *Law Enforcement Management and Administrative Statistics, 1997: Data for Individual State and Local Agencies with 100 or More Officers*, cited herein as "Reaves and Goldberg, 1999"; Reaves and Goldberg, *Local Police Departments 1997*, cited herein as "Reaves and Goldberg, 2000"; and Goldberg and Reaves, *Sheriffs' Departments 1997*, cited herein as "Goldberg and Reaves, 2000."

[2]For the LETS survey to local police, percentages have been statistically adjusted to represent the entire population. See Appendix A for a description of the adjustment methodology. For the LETS survey to state police and the FTS survey to crime labs, results are reported as unadjusted percentages.

workspace computers as "modern" or "state of the art," while 34 percent described theirs as "old but serviceable," and only 7 percent said theirs were "obsolete." All state police surveyed by RAND had computers in workspaces. Eighty-seven percent characterized their computers as "modern" or "state of the art" (LETS, 22g).

When examining whether computer technology had been brought into police patrol cars, RAND found that about two-thirds of urban departments serving populations greater than 75,000 did have computers in police cruisers, while somewhat less than half of the smaller urban departments and only 5 percent of rural departments have computers in cars. This is a very large gap between rural and other departments. Fifty-three percent of state police indicated they have computers in patrol cars.

Computerized Data and Networks

Computer Network and Remote Database Access

Because of the increase in capability that comes from networking computers and gaining access to centralized databases of information, it is of interest what fraction of the law enforcement community has these resources available. Among local police departments, those serving larger populations are more likely to have access to computer networks and to regional or national databases (LETS, 22). All state police responding to the RAND survey reported having computer networks available to their departments and all indicated that their agency had computer access to other regional or national databases (LETS, 22, 20).

Local Area Networks (LAN) and Wide Area Networks (WAN)

To gain a deeper understanding of the kinds of network resources that are available, the RAND survey also asked if departments had access to local area networks (LANs) or wide area networks (WANs). Almost all state police and better than half of local police departments have local area networks. Eighty percent of state police use wide area networks; however, only 18 percent of local police agencies report utilizing WANs. It should be noted, however, that depending on the needs of a department, a WAN might not be necessary or helpful to a local police force.

Integrated Data Systems

Another computer-based technology that can augment law enforcement effectiveness is the ability to integrate the many streams of data involved in police work. The RAND Law Enforcement Survey found that 41 percent of local police have integrated, computerized, crime/traffic/arrest data systems. Among local police, we found no significant differences between municipal/city and county police/sheriffs' departments in the percentage that had such systems. However, there were some significant differences across local police departments by size of population served. Between 30 and 40 percent of rural and urban departments serving populations less than 25,000 have integrated crime, traffic, and arrest data systems, as compared to 52–69 percent of the police departments in larger urban settings. Only 20 percent of state police reported having integrated crime/traffic/arrest data systems.

National Crime Information Center (NCIC)

The National Crime Information Center (NCIC) standards define an array of abilities a field officer should be able to perform electronically from a patrol car. A description of these functions and the databases to support them are included in the following text boxes. The RAND Law Enforcement Survey found 80 percent of state police and 62 percent of local police operate communications systems compliant with NCIC 2000 standards.

2000 Capabilities

When the NCIC 2000 system is complete and operational, a field officer in a patrol car will be able to:

- Enter a wanted person's fingerprint, mug shot, and identifying images;
- Identify a wanted person using a fingerprint;
- Modify a fingerprint entered into the system with a new fingerprint;
- Link a wanted person's fingerprint to one entered by another organization;
- Cancel a wanted person's fingerprint; and
- Receive ownership of a linked fingerprint when the original owner canceled the entry (Imel and Hart, 2000, p. 81).

The NCIC workstation and the mobile imaging unit (MIU) are based on Intel's Pentium technology. The FBI has published hardware and software requirements. The FBI will provide workstation applications software to the states at no cost (Imel and Hart, 2000, p. 82).

NCIC 2000 Databases

The FBI's National Crime Information Center (NCIC) 2000 began operations July 11, 1999, replacing the older system, in use since 1967. The NCIC 2000 system can process more than 2.4 million transactions a day, with storage of and access to more than 39 million records. The system will provide to local, state, and federal law enforcement agencies information organized in the following 17 databases: Canadian police information center, criminal history queries, criminal justice agency identifier, deported felons, foreign fugitives, gang and terrorist members, missing persons, persons subject to protection orders, stolen articles, stolen boats, stolen guns, stolen license plates, stolen securities, stolen vehicles, U.S. Secret Service protective file, unidentified persons, and wanted persons (FBI Press Release, July 15, 1999).

Priorities of Computer-Related Needs

In an effort to gauge the relative priority of the many potential information technology needs of police departments, the RAND Law Enforcement Survey asked respondents to characterize their needs for computer hardware, software, and training, Internet/e-mail access, and networked computers as high, medium, low, or not a priority. The survey instrument did not define these terms.

In comparing local police ratings across the computer-related needs as shown in Figure 2, what is most noticeable is that more departments see Internet/e-mail access and networked computers as a low/not a priority than is the case for computer hardware, software, and training. Furthermore, relatively few departments see Internet/e-mail access as a high priority need. The reason may be that departments have Internet access and locally networked computers and, as a result, they see less future need for them; this is consistent with the relatively high proportion of departments that report having networks (see above). On the other hand, there continues to be demand for additional hardware, software, and training. It may also be the case that departments value hardware, software, and training more than e-mail and network capabilities. It is interesting to note that even though 54 percent of respondents indicated their computers were modern or state of the art and 34 percent indicated

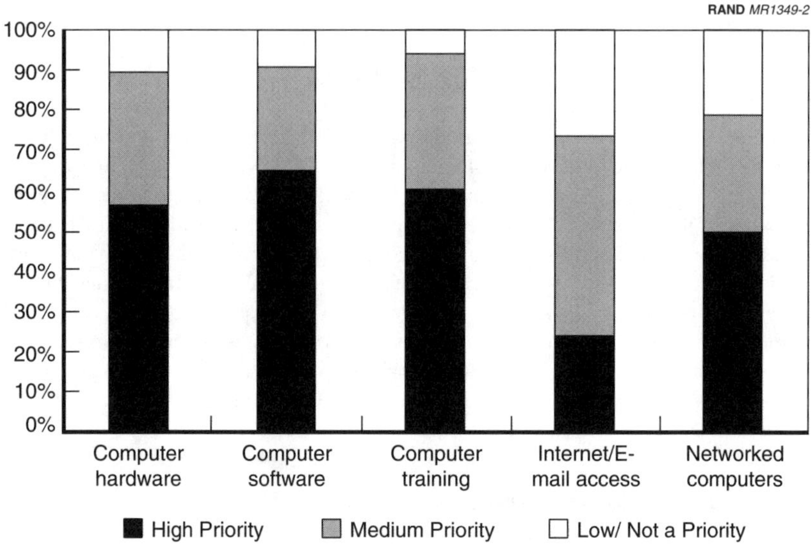

SOURCE: LETS, 11. Numbers are statistically adjusted percent of local departments that assigned the various priorities to needs.

Figure 2—Computer-Related Priorities of Local Police

they were old but serviceable (LETS, 22g), approximately 55 percent of the departments still indicate that computer hardware is a high priority. This finding emphasizes the importance of not just availability of computers but their quality as well.

In comparing each computer-related need by category of department by size of population served, what is most noticeable is that rural departments tend to assign higher priority to these needs than do urban departments. This observation is discussed more fully in the next section. Additionally, state police departments almost never assigned a need "low" or "no priority"; readers should not make too much of the state police responses, however, as the sample was small.

Closing the "Digital Divide"

In order to address the question of whether or not a digital divide exists between small and large law enforcement departments, the RAND Law Enforcement Survey asked about the availability of different digital technologies and the quality of those technologies. For this analysis, we grouped the different sizes of local police departments into two categories:[3]

- Rural and small departments (included rural departments and urban departments serving populations less than 25,000)
- Large departments (included urban departments serving populations greater than 25,000)

Do departments serving larger populations have significantly better digital technology than rural departments or urban departments serving smaller populations? In general, the answer is yes—supporting the assertion that there is a digital divide between large and small local police departments. To illustrate:

- A higher percentage of rural and small departments than larger departments indicate lack of availability of computers or digital technology.
- A greater percentage of rural and small departments than larger departments have either obsolete or old-but-serviceable computers in the workspace.
- For all categories, larger departments tend to have more modern computer equipment and technology than rural or small departments.

Given that there appears to be an actual digital divide, is it simply because those without extensive computerization perceive little or no need for it?

No. The RAND Law Enforcement Survey found that urban departments serving a population more than 25,000 did not differ signifi-

---

[3]These groupings were derived based on the results of regression analyses and t tests of statistical significance to determine whether the mean differences between strata were statistically significant or not. Differences were significant at $p<0.01$.

cantly from rural and small urban departments in their perceived need for computer or digital technology. Overall, about half of the large departments and half of the rural and small departments rated having networked computers within their agency as being a high priority. A quarter of large, rural, and small departments rated Internet/e-mail access as a high priority.

Broader Visions for Information Technology

Advances in information technology are important to local police forces for more reasons than just what they can do for the administration of the force. Taking a broader view of the issue, the IT revolution also requires changes in the way departments think about the "systems" within society with which they interact. These shifts in "systems thinking" are necessary so law enforcement can remain effective in light of the changes that IT is catalyzing in society and what those shifts mean for police missions and tasks. These changes in thinking require adjustment both above and below the level of the local department.

Above the level of the local police department, it is becoming increasingly clear that government agencies and governments as a whole need to take more holistic approaches to information technology. One noteworthy example of such is Kentucky's Unified Criminal Justice Information System (UCJIS),

> ... an information system that utilizes technology to capture electronically at the earliest opportunity data built on a set of unique identifiers (charge and individual). This data will appear as a seamless record of an individual's encounters with the criminal justice system. The mission of the UCJIS is to provide for the collection and availability of accurate up-to-date information relating to individuals charged with or convicted of a criminal offense in a timely and easily accessible manner to the criminal justice community while maintaining appropriate security and privacy standards.[4]

Other states with somewhat similar initiatives include Alaska, California, Colorado, Connecticut, Delaware, Florida, Georgia,

---

[4]See http://www.state.ky.us/agencies/ucjis/index.html.

Hawaii, Kansas, Maine, Massachusetts, Minnesota, Michigan, Nebraska, New Jersey, Pennsylvania, and Wisconsin.[5]

The Washington State Department of Corrections is developing an Offender Management Network Information (OMNI) system. When completed in 2005, the system is planned to include the following modules:

- Case File Audit,
- Case Management,
- CCO Workload/Assignment,
- Chemical Dependency,
- Chronos,
- Classification,
- Community Service,
- Cost of Supervision,
- Detainers & Warrants,
- Disciplinary & Violations/Sanctions,
- End of sentence review,
- Grievance,
- Indeterminate Sentence Review Board,
- Inmate Trust Accounting,
- Inmate Property Tracking,
- Interstate Compact/Border Administration,
- Legal Financial Obligations,
- Medical & Dental Records, Offender,
- Offender Groups,
- Offender Minimum Management Unit (OMMU),
- Pre-Sentence Investigation,

[5]For summary on the basic approach, agencies involved, organizational structure, and funding of these see http://www.bjis.state.wi.us and associated Web links.

- Public Access,
- Records,
- Release,
- Resource & Planning Management (RPM),
- Schedule,
- Sentence Structure & Time Accounting,
- Sex Offender Treatment Program, and
- Victim/Witness.

The system is the state's largest investment in information technology in recent years.[6] Wisconsin and California are undertaking or considering similar efforts. Such expansive, interconnected systems are designed on the premise that beyond sharing information with all parts of what is traditionally considered the law enforcement or criminal justice systems, there are benefits to facilitating appropriate information flow between the criminal justice system and education, social services, transportation, and other agencies or organizations.

It should be noted that there are often serious technical issues to interconnecting and promoting information exchange and use among different systems. These technical issues represent an important area of R&D if these transitions are to be facilitated. One example of a set of technical issues being sorted through can be found in the area of electronic legal documents. The era of legally recognized electronic documents is just beginning, but it has potential to improve convenience and reduce costs in many areas, including law enforcement and the criminal justice system. LegalXML,[7] a non-profit organization comprised of volunteer members from private industry, non-profit organizations, government, and academia, is developing open, non-proprietary technical standards for legal documents. There are many other efforts to use XML to facilitate sharing of information, much of which is supported by the federal community. Examples include a standard for electronic filing adopted by courts, a standard

[6]See http://www.wa.gov/dis/jin/comupdt12_99.htm.

[7]XML stands for Extensible Markup Language. For current information on this, search the World Wide Web for "XML" or "LegalXML."

for sharing of intelligence data, and a standard for sharing rap sheet information.

In addition to understanding the systems changes that must occur above the level of the local or state law enforcement department, information technology advance is catalyzing changes below the department level that are also important for police forces to consider. Since 1970, both computing power and communications capacity have been doubling every two years. The information revolution may continue at this rate for another decade or longer (Nichiporuk and Builder, 1995). The information revolution tends to weaken hierarchies—such as traditionally organized law enforcement agencies—through two processes:

- The shift from relative poverty to abundance in information permits individuals to bypass hierarchies that have—deliberately or inadvertently—controlled or limited information.
- Alternative human organizational forms—based mainly on the network—have proved more effective and efficient for transacting information than hierarchies. In information-intensive enterprises, hierarchical organizations may not be competitive with networks (Nichiporuk and Builder, 1995, p. 27).

This last point may become especially important to law enforcement if criminal enterprises adopt networked, rather than hierarchical, organization. Transnational criminal organizations are gaining strength partly because they are adept at building networks (Sterling, 1994). In this area, the change in society catalyzed by network-focused organization and activity could pose a serious threat to law enforcement in the near to mid term.

Although such network-focused organizations will pose a challenge to police forces, it is also possible that, by making changes in the way law enforcement operates, network arrangements can be adapted for the benefit of public safety. One example of this potential is found in Portland, Oregon. The Portland Police Bureau is strongly oriented toward community policing. As a result, ways in which networks and IT can facilitate and strengthen community policing is a high priority. Some examples of activities under consideration include:

> To improve information collection: issue a notebook computer to all personnel, install communications software on notebook computers and establish a live communications link in cars, install voice transcription software for incident reporting by officers, and improve processes for citizen crime reporting.
>
> To improve mutual information access: work to change any statutes that unnecessarily prohibit information sharing, work to overcome any organizational biases that inhibit sharing, and set up network mechanisms that allow all city agencies and schools to access portions of each other's management information systems.
>
> To disseminate information widely: post up-to-date, readily understandable crime data on the Portland Police Bureau website, and post information that shows what was done or learned after an incident was reported.
>
> To improve internal and external communication: make sure every employee has an Internet e-mail address, issue portable telephones to officers, establish a channel through which citizens could check on the status of crimes they reported, look into the possibility of using technology to free officers from frequent and lengthy trips to court, and use video technology to supplement (but not replace) face-to-face meetings (Institute for Law and Justice, 1999, pp. 24–28).

Such applications of technology, by strengthening the community and organizational networks on which good and responsive police work depend, could represent a way that a network-focused approach could result in increases in the effectiveness of police.

PLANNING

Tele- and Video-Conferencing

Just as is the case for all organizations whose members are not concentrated in a single geographic area, if teleconferencing (conference calls) and videoconferencing can substitute for some face-to-face meetings, then time and money spent traveling to meetings can be reduced and those resources can then be applied more productively.

The RAND survey found that 60 percent of local departments have conference call equipment that is "serviceable" or better, but only 10 percent have video conferencing equipment "serviceable" or better. All state police respondents have conference call equipment that is at least "serviceable," while one-third have modern or state-of-the-art videoconferencing equipment (the other two-thirds have none).

Likely due to their higher absolute demand for use of the technology, larger urban departments and state police are, in general, better equipped for conferencing.

RISK MANAGEMENT

In assessing the impact of risk perception on technology concerns of local law enforcement, it is relevant to examine the idea of risk along each of the three "axes" discussed earlier—liability/risk (traditional risk management), technological risk, and risk associated with public reactions.

Overall, the perceived risks associated with technologies from the perspective of liability varied greatly from technology to technology and differed for different-sized departments. The technologies for which risk/liability were most frequently identified as barriers to future adoption included handheld electrical devices (both direct and stand-off), flash grenades, tire deflation spikes, and rubber bullets. In examining how the perception of risk differed by the size of the population served, medium-sized departments (serving between 25,000 and 75,000 people) were most often the most concerned about individual technologies compared to either larger or smaller departments (LETS, 31,36).

Examining the perception of the operational risks associated with these technologies—based on departments' identifying reliability/effectiveness of the technology as a barrier to future acquisition—other interesting patterns present themselves. For most technologies, approximately 7 percent of local departments indicated that questions about reliability or effectiveness were a barrier. Three technologies stood out as markedly above this average value—smart guns (14 percent), electrical disruption devices for automobiles (11 percent), and tire deflation spikes (10 percent). Furthermore, these three technologies also represented the cases where there was the greatest divergence in the perceived risk between differently sized populations of departments. For example, while 35 percent of the largest urban departments indicated that this factor was a barrier to their acquisition of smart guns, only 10 percent of rural departments did so. In general, large departments were more concerned with technological risk than smaller departments (LETS, 31,36).

There was far more agreement on the public opinion linked risks associated with the technologies addressed on the RAND Police Survey. For most technologies, about 5 percent of local departments indicated that public opinion would be a barrier to future acquisition. The only two technologies that stood out markedly from this pattern were handheld electrical devices (both direct and stand-off) for which public opinion was cited by 11 and 13 percent of local departments respectively. There were few clear patterns in concern about public opinion based on size of jurisdiction though larger departments tended to consider it more of a factor than smaller ones. There was also little divergence in the percentages of different-sized departments that cited this factor for individual technologies. The one technology for which there was significant divergence was for stand-off electrical devices. Twenty percent of departments serving 25,000–75,000 people cited public opinion as a barrier to their acquisition while only 5 percent of departments serving 75,000–225,000 did so. The significance of this observation, if indeed it is significant, is unclear (LETS, 31,36).

TECHNOLOGY ACQUISITION

Because of the importance of information access in reducing the risks associated with adopting new technology, the perceived need for this type of information on the part of police organizations is of interest. The RAND survey asked respondents to rate their need for information to make better technology-related plans and decisions as high, medium, or low/no priority. Overall, 45 percent of local departments rated this as high priority, 48 percent as medium priority, and 7 percent as low/no priority. Among state police the percentages were 75, 17, and 8, respectively (LETS, 9a). Although this does indicate a much higher priority on the part of state police organizations on the availability of this information, it is noteworthy that only 7 percent of the local departments rated this as a low priority.

The survey also asked respondents to rate their need for standards by which equipment or other technology can be judged or certified.

Overall, 26 percent of local departments rated this as high priority, 59 percent as medium priority, and 16 percent as low/no priority. Among state police the percentages were 67, 25, and 8, respectively (LETS, 9); once again these results appear to indicate a closer focus on technology acquisition at the state police level. The only medium level of priority placed on technology standards by local police organizations is in conflict with discussions from focus group participants which considered reliable technology standards to be very important. It is also somewhat in conflict with the higher priority which local departments placed on interoperability (LETS, 9) since standards can support attempts to make technologies purchased by different departments interoperable. As a result, this somewhat anomalous result may depend on the calculus survey respondents applied to compare the abstract concept of "standards" to other more operational priorities and needs.

TRAINING

In the adoption of any new technology, integrating it into the operations of an organization is always an important step with respect to the real, long-term effect of the technology on organizational productivity or effectiveness. Without this integration process—the "human" portion of technology adoption—resources spent on even the most powerful technology are wasted since its intended users will not be able to apply it effectively. Because of the numerous possible functions of new technology, the relationships between technology and training in the law enforcement sphere is complex. At the minimum, at least three links between them can be identified, each with qualitatively different consequences:

1. People have to be trained to use technology. It is not uncommon for funding to be available to acquire technology without being available to train people to use it. In extreme cases the technology is unused because no one knows how to use it; in other cases it is underutilized because people are not trained to use its full capabilities. Here, increased supply of technology increases demand for training.

2. The purpose of some technology is to train people. Examples of such training technology include tutorial software and audio-

visual training aids. Here, increased supply of technology increases supply of training.

3. Technology can be designed to perform functions with minimal help from trained operators. Examples range from bar code scanners to robotic laboratory test equipment. Here, increased supply of technology decreases subsequent demand for training once routines and operations of the organization have been adapted to the new technology.

In all three of these cases, adoption of new technology will require a training period after the technology is introduced before its benefits are realized. It is through training that members of the organization are taught how to use new technology; by paying sufficient attention to the training process, the chance that any given resource investment in new technology will pay off can be greatly increased.

Current Availability of Training Technology and Technology Training

Because of its criticality in effective technology adoption, understanding the current availability of training resources in law enforcement is of significant importance.

Training Technology

Since advances in computer and other technologies can be applied to training tasks (potentially increasing the effectiveness or training or broadening the audience exposed to it), the RAND Law Enforcement Survey asked about the overall availability and the quality of the training technology currently in use by police departments.

From the responses to the survey, it appears that training equipment represents a significant technology shortfall in many departments. A number of departments indicated that computer-based training equipment (40 percent) and training equipment in general (27 percent), were not currently available to their staff. Only a few departments indicated that training equipment was not needed (LETS, 29).

Of those departments that had training technology in these two areas, only a quarter indicated that it was modern or state of the art.

Thirty-five percent of departments considered their training equipment and 21 percent considered their computer-based training equipment to be old but serviceable. One of out 10 departments reported having obsolete equipment both in terms of computer-based training equipment and training equipment in general.

Of the state police departments surveyed, most of them had training technology available to them. Unlike local police departments, a greater percentage of state-level departments indicated the quality of their computer and training technology was modern or state of the art.

Training Management Systems

Because of the challenge of managing the training programs of potentially complex departments, technology can also play a role in facilitating the task. While 40 percent of state police reported they have computerized training management systems, only 12 percent of local police have them (LETS, 16). It should be noted, however, that for many small departments (whose training programs are presumably easier to coordinate), such a system might not be necessary.

Future Needs Related to Training

Local law enforcement officials have consistently identified training as a major shortfall. Smaller departments, in particular, find it difficult to break away personnel to get the training they need. This cuts across all areas of law enforcement, including crime laboratories. When local or state law enforcement organizations seek training, several federal sources exist to provide it. The FBI is a major provider of training, the National Law Enforcement and Corrections Technology Centers provide training on crime mapping and other subjects, and the Department of Defense is becoming more involved in law enforcement training. Technology that can help provide training locally could be one way to approach this need.

In exploring this topic, the RAND survey asked respondents to rate their need for technology to more effectively or efficiently train personnel as high, medium, or low/no priority. Overall, 58 percent of local departments rated this as high priority, 35 percent as medium priority, and 6 percent as low/no priority. We found no significant differences among local police by urbanicity or size of population served. Among state police the percentages were 58, 41, and 0, respectively (LETS, 9e).

In addition, the survey also asked respondents to rate their need for training to use technology presently available or being acquired by their agency. Overall, 43 percent of local departments rated this as high priority, 43 percent as medium priority, and 14 percent as low/no priority. Urban departments were more likely to rate both types of training as being a high priority than rural departments. The larger the size of population served by a department, the more likely it was to assign a higher priority to training to use technology presently available to their department. Among state police the percentages were 50, 42, and 8, respectively (LETS, 9f). This demand for training on current technologies emphasizes that law enforcement organizations believe they are not adopting current technologies as effectively as they might and are therefore not gaining the maximal amount of benefit from them.

A third of local police departments felt that funding was a major contributing factor to their agency's training shortfalls. Lack of funding included insufficient budgets to cover training costs, equipment, or officers' salaries (including overtime and backfill pay). Eighteen percent of local police departments also cited a lack of time, manpower, or trainers as being a major training shortfall. Lack of time or manpower in this case refers to insufficient manpower to free up officers for training, or lack of time to allow officers to take "time-off" from regular duties to participate in training exercises (LETS, 10).

Computer training, which included both training to use computers (or software) and computer-based training (software and equipment), was viewed by only a small percentage of local police departments as being a training shortfall. Yet, as noted earlier, computer training at the same time was rated by two-thirds of local police as being a high priority with respect to their department's computer-related needs (LETS, 10).

Other training shortfalls mentioned included the unavailability of training locally. This category included reliance on other city or police departments to provide training, lack of space or facilities for training, lack of departmental in-service training capability, remote location of the department, and long travel distances necessary to attend training. About 2 percent of departments also mentioned keeping up with mandated training (including advances and changes in technology, legal updates, etc.) as being problematic (LETS, 10).

Other training shortfalls cited by local police included:

- A need for various forms of specialized training such as defensive tactics, community policing, telecommunications/communications operations, emergency vehicle and pursuit operations, 911 dispatchers, drug investigations, technology crimes (e.g., identity theft)
- A need for administrative-type training such as report writing and interviewing methods
- Lack of a centralized database to track agency-wide training
- A few local police also commented that training was not seen as an organizational priority within their agency (LETS, 10).

Perceived training shortfalls were somewhat related to urbanicity and size of population served. Rural and urban departments serving populations less than 25,000 were somewhat more likely to report lack of funding and less likely to cite availability of computer training and/or computer software as being major contributors to their agency's training shortfalls. For local police in large metropolitan areas (more than 225,000) lack of time, available manpower, and available trainers were the reasons mentioned most frequently as contributing any training shortfalls within their department (LETS, 10).

Similar to local police, 20 percent of state police departments indicated that lack of funding was an important contributing factor to any training shortfalls. Keeping up with mandated training and having to rely on other agencies for training were also cited (LETS, 10).

Interviewees also indicated that there is a tremendous amount of duplication of curricula with little effort being made to develop standards with respect to curricula.

Training as a Factor Limiting Technology Acquisition

Overall, training was among the top three factors cited by local and state-level departments as influencing acquisition decisions. As would be expected given the significant differences among them, how important training requirements are in terms of influencing future acquisition decisions or usage of different policing and less-than-lethal weapons technologies varied. Here, we summarize the findings as reported in Chapter 2 (Crime Prevention) and Chapter 3 (First Response).

With respect to different types of policing technologies:

- Relatively few local police (less than 10 percent) felt that training requirements were an important factor with respect to the use of video cameras either in patrol cars or in fixed or mobile surveillance.
- Only 10 percent of departments considered training to be key with respect to acquisition of night vision/electro-optic devices, smart guns, and for most vehicle stopping/tracking devices (tire deflation spikes, stolen vehicle tracking) and digital imaging devices (fingerprints, mug shots).
- The exceptions were electrical/engine disruption devices and suspect composites where as many as 20 percent of local police viewed training requirements as influencing the use or acquisition of these devices.
- State police organizations surveyed saw training as relatively more important than local forces. The percentage of state organizations citing training as a factor went as high as 47 percent for handheld electrical devices.

The importance of training requirements with respect to future acquisition decisions showed no clear trends by size of population served by local police. The exception was in terms of use of tire deflation spikes: Rural departments were less likely to view training as being important—possibly as a function of lesser need for these devices. Conversely, large urban (greater than 225,000) departments were more likely to view training as being important—again, perhaps reflecting greater usage of these devices by these departments.

Medium- to large-sized departments were more likely to view training as being important with respect to mobile or fixed-site surveillance, tire deflation spikes, and for most digital imaging devices. These departments were less likely to view training requirements as a limiting factor for night vision devices or other types of vehicle-stopping devices (e.g., electrical/engine disruption and stolen vehicle tracking).

Approximately one out of five local departments viewed training as a factor limiting future acquisition or use of less-than-lethal (LTL) devices. In particular, a quarter of local police across all size categories considered training requirements to be a limiting factor for use of flash/bang grenades. Whereas, the other types of devices or agents showed more variation in terms of relative importance placed on training. There was no clear pattern seen by size of population served in terms of training being viewed as a key factor influencing use or acquisition of the other types of LTL weapons or devices included in the survey. The exception was use of pepper spray where rural departments or those departments serving urban populations 75,000 or less were somewhat more likely to view training as being a limiting factor with respect to usage.

With the exception of pepper spray, about one-third of state police departments considered training requirements as being a limiting factor in the use or acquisition of LTL devices. These departments tended to view training as being somewhat more important with respect to the use of blunt trauma/soft projectile devices and flash/bang grenades than for the other devices listed.

Forensic Science Education

Education in forensic sciences is offered at several colleges and universities across the country, but their programs vary in scope and content. Programs are housed in various academic departments; a forensics program in a chemistry department, for example, may well emphasize forensic chemistry but may not cover other forensic theory and methods in the same depth. As a result, newly graduated forensic scientists must spend a year or two in on-the-job training to become fully qualified.

Furthermore, many labs cannot afford recommended levels of continuing education and in-service training. Of those survey respondents reporting a separate training budget, the average amount was $1,102 per technical staff member; however, this can be misleading because there is great variability in funding available for training, ranging from zero to more than $2,000 per testifying examiner. ASCLD recommends each technical staff member receive $1,000 in continuing education training annually; of the labs that reported training budget information, more than 60 percent indicated that they budget less than this recommended amount per staff member.

Distance Learning

The U.S. Army is currently implementing a large-scale distance learning program, which calls for converting portions of hundreds of courses to distance learning, at a total cost of about $840 million for infrastructure and courseware development over a 13-year period. Proponents of distance learning expect its benefits to include:

- Lower costs to agencies offering and receiving courses, once the courseware is developed,
- Less time away from students' normal workplace duties, and
- Increased training capacity.

Distance learning strategies could represent an approach to meeting the training needs of departments or laboratories whose employees must fit training around operational commitments or are too remote to make traveling to training opportunities practical.

ACCOUNTABILITY

The highest calling of those who enforce our laws is not to be masters of technology but servants of justice. It is increasingly clear, however, that technology has a role to play in such service.[8] Justice requires that law enforcement be accountable to agency leadership and to the public. As videotaping of the Rodney King beating and subsequent

---

[8]See, for example, Scheck et al. (2000) quoted in Chapter 5.

incidents have shown, technology *will* play a role in making law enforcement accountable.

Technology can be beneficial both in serving to deter and/or document police abuses of power and to provide objective evidence of proper police actions if wrongful accusations are made against officers. Technology can be abused, however, if surveillance technologies are used to violate reasonable standards of personal privacy, if polygraph or other investigative technologies are used oppressively, or if crowd control technologies are used to suppress peaceful dissent. On the other hand, technology can help make police-public confrontations less volatile and can help make review of police use of force more effective, objective, and accepted.

Among respondents to the RAND survey, the larger local, as well as the state, departments ranked technology for improving accountability as high priority (Table 22). As might be expected, agencies that serve larger publics tend to rate this a higher priority than those with fewer people in their jurisdictions (LETS, 9).

Accountability to Police Leadership

In addition to accounting for their actions to the citizens they serve, police commanders also must be accountable to those higher in their organizations. One central component of that process is collection of accurate data on crime incidence that is used to both guide and justify activities intended to reduce its level. The RAND survey found 23

Table 22

Stated Priority of Technology for Improving Accountability Within Agency

Population Served	Low/Not Priority	Medium Priority	High Priority
Rural	16%	47%	37%
Urban <25K	5%	46%	49%
Urban 25–75K	7%	48%	45%
Urban 75–225K	6%	42%	52%
Urban >225K	5%	30%	64%
All Local Police	8%	46%	46%
State Police	0%	27%	73%

SOURCE: LETS, 9d. Numbers are statistically adjusted percent of departments.

percent of local police stating they use crime mapping and analysis for command review and planning of operations (Table 23). The larger the population a department serves, the more likely it is to do crime mapping and analysis. A relatively small percentage of local police use formal crime-mapping techniques or process similar to New York City's COMPSTAT[9] or Los Angeles' FASTRAC,[10] as compared to the more widespread use of less formal or automated processes. About one-third of state police indicate that they use crime mapping and analysis for command review and planning of operations. Most of these departments use a less formal or automated process than what is currently being used in New York City or Los Angeles (LETS, 21).

In comparison, about one-third of state police indicate that they use crime mapping and analysis for command review and planning of

Table 23

Crime Mapping and Analysis by Local Police, by Population Served

Population Served	Yes, department does crime mapping and analysis	Less formal crime mapping techniques used	Formal crime mapping techniques used
Rural	14%	12%	1%
Urban <25K	20%	18%	2%
Urban 25–75K	34%	31%	3%
Urban 75–225K	57%	52%	6%
Large Urban >225K	69%	44%	23%
Overall Local	23%	20%	2%
State	33%	7%	27%

SOURCE: LETS, 21. Numbers are statistically adjusted percents of local police indicating use of crime mapping and analysis for command review and planning of operations.

---

[9]COMPSTAT has four key components: (1) accurate and timely intelligence, (2) rapid deployment, (3) effective tactics, and (4) follow-up and assessment. Crime data collection and mapping are crucial to the first of these components.

[10]FASTRAC stands for "focus, accountability, teamwork, response, and coordination," the Los Angeles Police Department's command accountability model for results-oriented policing. Crime trends and patterns are tracked daily using computerized statistical databases, and area commanders meet weekly with the Chief and senior managers to discuss their efforts to reduce Part I crimes.

operations. Most of these departments use a less formal or automated process than what is currently being used in New York City or Los Angeles. About 20 percent of state police geocode and map either incidents or hot spots; while 13 percent also geocode calls for service and arrests (LETS, 24).

Video Cameras in Patrol Cars

Among state and local law enforcement agencies the most common use of video cameras is in patrol cars. Video cameras in patrol cars can provide credible evidence against lawbreakers, as well as evidence for or against police accused of abusive behavior. In 1997, 46 percent of all larger local police departments with 100 or more officers were found to be using video cameras in patrol cars (Reaves and Goldberg, 1999, p. xvii). By 2000, 62 percent of these departments made some use of this technology.

Among local police department of *all* sizes, RAND found 15 percent making widespread use of patrol car video camera surveillance, with 30 percent making limited use of this technology, and 55 percent not using it at all. Among state police, 33 percent reported making widespread use of the technology, with the remaining 67 percent reporting limited use (LETS, 36c).

In general, the larger urban departments are more likely to be using video cameras in patrol cars. The exception is the estimate that only 8 percent of departments serving populations greater than 225,000 use video cameras in patrol cars. The reason for this deviation is unclear, though it may be that these departments operate so many units that widespread outfitting of patrol cars proves cumulatively too expensive.

Unlike local police, all of the state police reported using video cameras in their patrol cars, with one-third indicating widespread usage.

Overwhelmingly, most local police considered cost to be the factor limiting future acquisition of video camera surveillance equipment. Rural and urban departments serving populations less than 25,000 were more likely than larger departments to consider cost a limiting factor. This is not surprising given the demand for the technology is undoubtedly much less in jurisdictions with fewer interactions between citizens and police and fewer criminal incidents. When judging a trade-off between patrol car cameras and other investments, these departments would certainly judge the relative weights differently than organizations in which the pay-off to video is higher. Relatively few local police (less than 10 percent) considered training requirements or reliability to be important factors influencing acquisition decisions. This is also not unexpected given the characteristics of the technology.

Similarly, three-quarters of state police departments surveyed considered cost to be the single most important factor limiting future acquisition of video camera surveillance equipment.

Internet Use

The posting of information on the Internet is one route organizations can take to make their operations more transparent and accessible to the public. RAND found that almost 60 percent of local police departments use the Internet to allow the public to communicate with their department via e-mail, and half of departments use the Internet to provide general information about the department (Table 24). Sixteen percent use the Internet to provide the public with information about crime statistics or crime maps showing the location of recent incidents. In addition, 9 percent of departments use the Internet to gather general information (including sharing of information with other agencies) or information specific to criminal activity (e.g., sexual predators, missing persons, or fugitives). A quarter of all local police do not use the Internet at all (LETS, 17).

Internet usage varies among local police by size of population served. In general, rural and urban departments serving populations less than 25,000 are less likely to use the Internet than larger departments. The larger departments were more likely than rural or small urban departments to use the Internet to allow individuals to communicate via e-mail with their department or to provide general information about their agency.

Table 24

Internet Use by Local Police

Internet Use	Overall	Rural	Urban (<25K)	Urban (25K–75K)	Urban (75K–225K)	Large Urban (>225K)
Allow individuals to communicate via e-mail with department	59%	64%	49%	89%	78%	83%
Provide general information about the department	50%	42%	44%	75%	80%	96%
Provide crime maps/crime statistics	16%	7%	16%	21%	36%	50%
Does not use the Internet	24%	20%	32%	7%	11%	1%

SOURCE: LETS, 17. Numbers are statistically adjusted percentage of local police indicating for what purpose(s) they use the Internet.

Civil Rights

Because it was deemed to be insufficiently accountable to the community on civil rights issues, the Los Angeles Police Department (LAPD) has been put under a consent decree by the Department of Justice that requires the city to build a computerized system for tracking police officers' activities. The system is expected to cost millions of dollars. The Pittsburgh Bureau of Police, under a similar federal decree, has a comparable system. In addition, the LAPD is being required to collect data on the ethnicity and gender of people subjected to traffic and pedestrian stops, to assess whether there is bias in selecting whom to detain (Newton and Daunt, 2000).

Just as pervasive surveillance through CCTV or other technology can be resented by the public, systems designed to improve officers' accountability to citizens and improve discipline can cause resentment within law enforcement agencies. For example, in the Los Angeles Police Department the newly introduced complaint system "is rejected as unfair by most officers, [contributing] to the disciplinary system's lack of legitimacy" (Wilms, Schmidt, and Norman, 2000, p. 66). LAPD's FASTRAC, inspired by New York's COMPSTAT, is intended to help top management audit crime patterns and departmental operations. Instead the system is said to "have reduced captains' ability to make decisions because they are, as one officer put it, 'always looking over their shoulders to see what the Chief wants'" (Wilms, Schmidt, and Norman, 2000, p. 27).

In marked similarity to the concerns expressed by officers with respect to monitoring and tracking technologies, these same issues can generate public concerns over what may seem to be the most benign and beneficial technologies. For example, there is a technology called ShotSpotter, currently being field tested, that senses the sound of gunshots and triangulates to determine gunshot location. Despite the fact that the technology is designed only to pick up sound characteristic of gunshots, people at community meetings have complained, "you have these sensors out there, and you hear everything we're saying—and we have a problem with that." An officer's private response to this (in contrast to police objections to monitoring cited above) was, "if the part of the community that's violating the law thinks that we can hear them, we don't have a problem with that." We also note that many people welcome ShotSpotter's potential for reducing random gunfire in their neighborhoods.

Use of Force Tracking Systems

To assess the breadth of application of another civil rights related administrative technology, the RAND Law Enforcement Survey asked how many departments had systems to track the lethal and nonlethal use of force by officers. The survey found 40 percent of state police have such a computerized system. In contrast, only 7 percent of local police reported having such systems (LETS, 16).

Complaint Management Systems

The Los Angeles Police Department's Board of Inquiry into the Rampart Area corruption incident made 108 recommendations for improving performance and accountability of the department. Implementation of many of these could be made less costly and burdensome through use of appropriate advanced technology. Specifically, one calls for review of the LAPD's "automated systems to determine if they are able to capture and produce information which may be required for effective audits and corruption investigations. For example, the Police Arrest and Crime Management Information System (PACMIS) database (or its successor, CCAD) must allow for retrieval of information on all officers involved in any given arrest" (Board of Inquiry, 2000).

To determine how widespread the use of such complaint systems was among state and local police, the topic was included in the RAND survey. Among respondents to the RAND Law Enforcement Survey, 60 percent of state police have a computerized complaint management system supporting Internal Affairs or the Inspector General, while only 7 percent of local police have such systems (LETS, 16).

Public Opinion and Privacy Issues

Respondents to the RAND Law Enforcement Survey considered public opinion to be least important in terms of influencing future acquisition decisions across all categories of policing technology devices and agents. However, large departments were more likely than smaller departments to cite public opinion as being key across all categories of policing technologies.

It is important to note, however, that while public opinion may not be a current concern, police use of technology is an area that has the potential to generate significant reactions from citizens. As a result, the salience of public opinion as a technology decisionmaking criterion could change rapidly. For the sake of example, use of databases containing personal information is becoming an increasingly salient issue to members of the public. A survey commissioned by the Bureau of Justice Statistics found 90 percent of adult Americans are concerned about possible misuse of personal information. Some 22 percent claim to have been a victim of an improper invasion of privacy by law enforcement or government tax, social service, welfare, or license agencies. Of those surveyed, 66 percent distinguish between access to *conviction* records and access to records of persons arrested but not convicted. Eighty-nine percent consider it very important to have a right to review their records and have errors corrected (Opinion Research Corporation International, 2000). As a result, it is critical for police organizations to remain cognizant of what the public considers appropriate law enforcement activity. If they do not, the potential always exists for individuals of groups to seek recourse via litigation or the political process for behavior—either technological or otherwise—that they deem inappropriate.[11]

---

[11]See, for example, Human Rights Watch (1998).

Part II

FEDERAL CHALLENGES AND CHOICES

Part II

FEDERAL CHALLENGES AND CHOICES

POLICY BACKGROUND

Under the American federal system most law is cast as state statutes and local ordinances; accordingly, most law enforcement is the responsibility of state and local agencies. Federal law and federal law enforcement come into play only where there is rationale for it, consistent with the Constitution. Within this framework, a clear role has been identified for federal support of state and local agencies. A major area of such support is technology-related with activities taking the following forms:

- Sponsoring research and development (R&D),
- Testing and evaluating technology and developing performance standards for technology and its use,
- Funding and otherwise assisting with acquisition of or access to technology,
- Providing training in the use of technology and developing technology used in training,
- Providing technology assistance by applying federal technology and expertise to specific problems, and
- Providing information on technology and its use in law enforcement.

Early Federal Initiatives

Over the last few years the federal government has demonstrated that it has a clear interest in supporting the development and deployment of new technologies for law enforcement. This is not the first time that the federal government has shown such an interest. The issue of law enforcement technology played a prominent role in the 1967 report of the President's Commission on Law Enforcement and Administration of Justice. At that time the Commission's report stated:

> ...the scientific and technological revolution that has so radically changed most of American society during the post few decades has had surprisingly little impact upon the criminal justice system. In an age when many executives in government and industry, faced with decisionmaking problems, ask the scientific and technical community for independent suggestions on possible alternatives and for objective analyses of possible consequences of their actions, the public officials responsible for establishing and administering the criminal law—the legislators, police, prosecutors, lawyers, judges and corrections officials—have almost no communication with the scientific and technical community. ...The police with crime laboratories and radio networks made early use of technology, but most police departments could have been equipped 30 or 40 years ago as well as they are today.

In response to the Commission's overall findings Congress passed the Omnibus Crime Control and Safe Streets Act of 1968, which created the Law Enforcement Assistance Administration (LEAA) and the National Institute of Law Enforcement and Criminal Justice (NILECJ). While LEAA provided law enforcement grants for, among other things, procuring new equipment, the NILECJ was to serve as a law enforcement R&D agency.

Despite the intent of these congressional actions and the expenditure of more than $31 million by 1977, little progress was made in bringing science and technology to bear for law enforcement. In fact, Congress was so disappointed in performance of LEAA that it dismantled the organization in 1979 and reorganized NILECJ to establish the National Institute of Justice (NIJ).[1] Despite previous interest in helping provide new technologies to law enforcement, there was little focus on technology within the new institute. With the exception of a few small, but significant developments such as the development of the national 911 system and bullet-resistant armor, little had changed in the tools being used by the law enforcement community.

A major reason for the persistence of this problem lay in the fact that the overwhelming majority of the more than 18,000 law enforcement agencies in this country are small in size. Approximately 90 percent of those agencies have 25 or fewer officers, with about 50 percent of them having 12 or fewer officers. As a result, the law enforcement community faced three problems in obtaining new technologies:

1. Law enforcement agencies had little if any in-house capabilities to find or assess commercial technologies that meet their needs.
2. Law enforcement agencies had virtually no in-house capability to conduct research and development or to test and evaluate new technologies that they might be interested in.
3. Most law enforcement agencies lacked resources to procure new technologies.

More Recent Initiatives

It is these areas that the federal government began to address more seriously. While funding has not yet reached the levels required to truly modernize our nation's law enforcement, the actions taken by the federal government have demonstrated clear interest in this area.

---

[1]The National Institute of Justice, a component of the Office of Justice Programs, is the research agency of the U.S. Department of Justice. NIJ is authorized to support research, evaluation, and demonstration programs, development of technology, and both national and international information dissemination. NIJ's Office of Science and Technology provides federal, state, and local law enforcement and corrections agencies access to the best technologies available and helps them develop capabilities essential to improving efficiency and effectiveness. One of the primary mechanisms through which the Office accomplishes this mission is its network of regional science and engineering support centers—the National Law Enforcement and Corrections Technology Centers. The Office also supports the development of new technologies to serve the needs of law enforcement and corrections agencies.

The first more recent recognition by Congress of the need for new law enforcement technology came in 1989 with the establishment of the CounterDrug Technology Assessment Center (CTAC) as an arm of the Office of National Drug Control Policy (ONDCP). CTAC was created to research and develop new technologies that can be used by federal, state, and local law enforcement in the war against drugs. Although limited in its scope and funding, the establishment of CTAC was the first concrete step toward providing law enforcement with technology support since the dismantling of LEAA.

At the end of 1992 NIJ created the Office of Science and Technology (OST), with a mission of assisting state and local law enforcement identify and access new technologies and a total budget of $2.3 million. The Office of Science and Technology is the only existing capability to support law enforcement's research and development interests in technologies such as the development of concealed weapons detection; creation of a successful smart gun; improvements in police body armor; better communications systems for law enforcement agencies, capable of operating across jurisdictional boundaries; and development of guides for the handling and protection of evidence in arson or bombing cases, homicides, or electronic crimes. It does this by funding research directly and by partnering with Defense and Energy Department projects, thus leveraging taxpayer investments.

By 1994, as Congress was considering the Crime Act, there was still little in the way of new technologies being adopted by the broader law enforcement community, particularly at the state and local level. The reason for this was simple—there were still not sufficient resources to help law enforcement address the three impediments identified above.

This began to change in 1994 in several ways. As Congress was considering the Crime Act, NIJ signed a Memorandum of Understanding with the Department of Defense to establish the Joint Program Steering Group, a joint program office to adapt technologies for the dual use of law enforcement and military peacekeeping forces.

During this same period Congress began to increase NIJ's budget to $13 million. This enabled NIJ to begin establishing the National Law Enforcement and Corrections Technology Center system (NLECTC) and the Justice Information Technology Network (JUSTNET). Both of these programs were established to begin addressing two of the impediments.

The NLECTC system would provide technical assistance concerning new technologies to law enforcement agencies. Until the creation of the NLECTCs, the only real technology assistance available to state and local organizations came either from within or from federal agencies that were themselves so strapped for resources that local agencies often waited for months or years for help, or were rejected altogether because the needed capability simply didn't exist. Further, federal agencies often have different needs, equipment, and capabilities than local agencies and so cannot offer some of the basic technology assistance needed, such as how to take advantage of surplus federal property; how to assemble a computer graphic presentation of a prosecutor's case; where to locate a metallurgist to help in a homicide investigation; or where to find test or certification results for body armor, police cars, or other equipment.

JUSTNET would provide them with information on new technologies and point them to test and evaluation information. While the resources provided were not sufficient to provide the levels of support needed by state and local law enforcement, the budget increase indicated that Congress was beginning to understand the need for this kind of support.

Despite the modesty of their budgets, these initiatives have successfully leveraged major technology investments already made by the American taxpayer. They have helped move millions in federal surplus property directly, by alerting agencies to the existence of useful equipment, and by teaching them how to access the system. They have provided thousands of technical publications and have even helped agencies design effective communications systems or develop electronic crime squads.

Also during the mid-1990s, at the instigation of numerous state and local law enforcement representatives, Congress amended the Community Oriented Policing Services (COPS) program plan to add funding for the COPS Making Officers Redeployment Effective (COPS MORE) program, to provide grants to law enforcement agencies to buy equipment and technologies. Congress directed that up to 20 percent of the total monies provided to COPS be made available for that purpose. Because it addressed a serious need, COPS MORE was very well received by the law enforcement community.

The federal government's interest in providing support for law enforcement technology continued following the passage of the Crime Act. In FY 1996 Congress appropriated more than $500 million for the Local Law Enforcement Block Grant (LLEBG) program, which, among other uses, permitted agencies to obtain funding for new equipment.[2] The LLEBG augmented already existing grant programs—most notably the Bryne Grant programs—administered by the Bureau of Justice Assistance (BJA) part of the Office of Justice Programs (OJP).

To make certain that new technologies were being developed and tested for law enforcement agencies, Congress set aside 1 percent of that funding, approximately $20 million, for NIJ's research and development program. Congress also increased the funding for the NLECTC system by more than $2 million. The result of these actions was to begin to institutionalize the NIJ technology program.

Over the next several years the upward trend increased as Congress and the Administration moved to increase their support for law enforcement technology. For example, in 1997 Congress passed the Counterterrorism and Effective Death Penalty Act, which appropriated an additional $10 million a year for two years to NIJ for the de-

---

[2]The Local Law Enforcement Block Grants (LLEBG) Program provides units of local government with funds to underwrite projects designed to reduce crime and improve public safety. Under the statutory provisions of the LLEBG Program, BJA sets aside funds to be awarded directly to units of local government within a state. BJA directly awards LLEBG funds to larger communities. The remaining funds in each state are distributed to individual programs and agencies by the chief executive officer.

The amounts awarded are proportionate to the state's average annual number of Part 1 violent crimes reported to the Federal Bureau of Investigation compared to the average for all other states for the three most recent calendar years. However, each state receives a minimum award of 0.25 percent of the total amount available for formula distribution.

By law, projects under this program must be funded in accordance with the following purpose areas: supporting law enforcement, enhancing security measures in and around schools, establishing or supporting drug courts, enhancing the adjudication of violent offenders, establishing multijurisdictional law enforcement task forces, enhancing crime prevention programs, and defraying the costs of indemnification insurance (http://www.ojp.usdoj.gov/BJA/html/llebg1.htm).

velopment of technologies to assist local agencies in combating terrorism. In 1998 Congress began to address new technology issues with new funding. At that time they provided $18 million to the Department of Justice for the training and equipping of public safety "first responders." This was increased to $75.5 million for FY 1999. Also in 1998, Congress adopted a $25 million Bulletproof Vest Partnership program to provide law enforcement officers with soft body armor. In addition, $10 million was earmarked from existing funds for the development of technologies to increase safety and security in schools.

Starting about 1998, the White House Office of Science and Technology Policy (OSTP), working with other federal agencies, began a serious examination of technology initiatives to fight crime. OSTP is currently encouraging a dialogue on how science and technology can support society's needs, with particular emphasis on the criminal justice system (Moore, 2000). This report both draws on insights emerging from that dialogue and seeks to make a contribution to it.

By FY 2000 the money devoted to law enforcement technology of one kind of another reached significant, although not necessarily sufficient, proportions. In FY 2000 the funding for NIJ's technology program increased to $129 million. The dollars available for first responder equipment purchases in FY 2000 increased to $85 million. Congress also appropriated $130 million for the Crime Identification Technology Act, which was designed to assist law enforcement in improving its information systems and forensic science capabilities. Congress also added a COPS Technology program to the COPS portfolio, funding it at approximately $100 million since FY 1999.

While the trend in increased federal support for law enforcement technology is significant, there is an important caveat to keep in mind as one looks at these numbers. A significant percentage of the funds appropriated for law enforcement technology has been earmarked for a specific programmatic use or for specific projects. For example, of the funds appropriated to NIJ's Office of Science and Technology for FY 2000, approximately 70 percent has been earmarked for specific purposes. About 80 percent of the approximately $100 million provided for the COPS Technology program was also earmarked in FY 2000. While one can debate the value of earmarks, they do, by definition, mean that fewer resources are available for competitive grant programs or discretionary use by the funding agency.

The issue of earmarking not withstanding, Congress has continued to express an interest in providing funding for technology for law enforcement uses. For example, in FY 2000 several members of Congress introduced legislation to increase the amount of funding for law enforcement technology.[3] Congress also acted to provide more support to the forensic science community.[4]

At the same time, during the Clinton administration, the Executive branch demonstrated a serious interest in increasing support for law enforcement technology. The White House Office of Science and Technology is helping to develop a "Crime Technology Initiative" designed to provide a programmatic framework for increased support.

In light of the now established federal role and involvement in law enforcement science and technology, discussion will now turn to examining responses to technology adoption barriers divided into the three classes introduced above—sources of technology-related information; research, development, and deployment; and technology application.

---

[3]Representatives Sherwood Boehlert (R-NY) and Bart Stupak (D-MI) introduced the Law Enforcement Science and Technology Act of 2000 to expand the NIJ Office of Science and Technology program by establishing a separate law enforcement technology program office in the Office of Justice Programs and providing $200 million a year in funding for that office.

[4]For example, the National Forensics Science Improvement Act (renamed the Paul Coverdall Memorial Forensics Science Improvement Act) was introduced by Senators Coverdall (R-GA) and Jeff Sessions (R-AL) to provide more than $500 million for the improvement of state and local crime laboratories.

Chapter Seven

SOURCES OF TECHNOLOGY INFORMATION AND SUPPORT

Before any organization, law enforcement or otherwise, can adopt a new technology, it must become aware of its existence and its capabilities. This awareness can come from many sources in both the public and private sectors ranging from word-of-mouth contact with peers to the advertising produced by technology vendors. Once basic information has been obtained about a new or unfamiliar technology, the individuals responsible for technology procurement must generally begin a learning process to gain a better understanding of the technology's capabilities and limitations. Allocation of scarce resources in any situation always implies opportunity costs and the more information that can be gathered before the purchase decision, the less the risk that costs and benefits will be misunderstood and investments will be made unwisely. Because of the interest in understanding the technology needs and decision processes of law enforcement agencies, gaining insight into the sources of technology information—both before an investment is made or afterward as support—is very important.

Major findings in this chapter include:

- Law enforcement organizations utilize many disparate sources to gather information regarding technology. While most state police organizations regularly utilize federal information sources, many local police forces do not. This observation suggests that more could potentially be done to make federal technology information resources more accessible to local police organizations.
- Local police forces seek technology-related support from many sources. Based on the results of the RAND survey, it appears that

organizations most frequently seek support in-house and at the local or state level before seeking federal assistance. Both the sources of support utilized by local law enforcement and the number of organizations that seek outside support at all differ depending on the specific technology or technique involved.

SOURCES OF TECHNOLOGY INFORMATION

Law enforcement agencies may draw on many possible sources of technology information. Results of the RAND Law Enforcement Survey suggest that state police commonly make use of more sources of information than do local departments. Table 25 delineates the percentages of local police departments indicating their agencies usually obtain information about law enforcement technology from each of the various sources listed.

As would be expected, commercial communication in magazines, from manufacturers, or at trade shows is very important; similarly, contact with colleagues also represents a very important source of information. Of particular interest are the values for utilization of the federal NLECTCs and Law Enforcement Online, arguably the most impartial and technically rigorous information sources included on the list. While a large fraction of state police organizations regularly use these resources, only about one in five local departments usually use them. This relatively low utilization could reflect a number of issues. It is possible that local departments seek information locally first and only continue the search to the federal level if satisfactory information is not available from other sources. Conversely, this could reflect the level of awareness of the federal information sources within local departments; if this is the case, it is possible that additional promotion of the resources that are available would lead additional local departments to take advantage of them.

SOURCES OF TECHNOLOGY-RELATED SUPPORT

Technology-related support—a much broader term encompassing more than simply the provision of information—is also an important input into state and local departments' technology base and

Table 25

Sources of Technology Information Used by Police

Sources of Information	Local Police	State Police
Magazines	83%	92%
Manufacturers	66%	92%
Word-of-mouth	66%	92%
Other law enforcement agencies/colleagues	64%	100%
Internet	54%	100%
Trade shows	40%	75%
Electronic bulletin boards	20%	67%
NLECTCs	18%	75%
Law Enforcement Online (LEO)	17%	42%

SOURCE: LETS, 33. Numbers are percent of police departments stating their agency usually obtains information about law enforcement technology from sources indicated. Local police numbers have been statistically adjusted to reflect the overall population of U.S. departments.

technical activities. Such support can include science and technology advice, aid in the performance of analyses, and training. In addition to contributing to ongoing investigations or problems, such activities also serve to convey information about technological options and their capabilities. Overall, 62 percent of local police indicated that they had received technology-related support from either in-house departments or from external agencies within the past year.[1] Some 83–87 percent of larger urban departments serving populations larger than 75,000 reported receiving some form of federal technology-related support during the past year. The percentage for smaller urban departments of 25,000–75,000 ranged from 62 to 67 percent. Fifty-one percent of rural departments reported receiving federal support (LETS, 32).

Table 26 shows percentages of local departments reporting that they received specific technology-related support from various sources. From the federal perspective what is most remarkable about these

[1] For the LETS survey to local police, percentages have been statistically adjusted to represent the entire population. See Appendix A for a description of the adjustment methodology. For the LETS survey to state police and the FTS survey to crime labs, results are reported as unadjusted percentages.

Table 26

Percent of Local Departments Receiving Technology-Related Support from Various Sources Within Past Year

Support	In-House	Local Agency	State Agency	Manu-facturer	NLECTC	FBI	ATF	Nat'l Labs	Other
Firearms tests	35%	16%	9%	9%	4%	4%	3%	1%	2%
Technology assistance[a]	32%	26%	19%	16%	7%	6%	5%	1%	3%
Training	59%	58%	46%	19%	16%	7%	7%	1%	4%
Audio evidence enhancement or analysis	16%	6%	5%	5%	2%	2%	1%	0%	1%
Video evidence enhancement or analysis	17%	12%	11%	11%	6%	4%	1%	0%	1%
Trace evidence analysis	49%	11%	9%	7%	2%	2%	1%	0%	1%
Technology testing and evaluations	15%	13%	8%	6%	5%	3%	2%	0%	1%
Cybercrime investigation or analysis	24%	14%	14%	2%	1%	0%	0%	0%	0%

SOURCE: LETS, 32. Numbers are statistically adjusted percent of departments reporting they received technology-related support from indicated sources in the past year.

[a]Technology assistance includes science and engineering advice and support.

findings is the small percentage of departments reporting receiving support from federal agencies—be they the National Law Enforcement and Corrections Technology Centers (NLECTC), Federal Bureau of Investigation (FBI), Bureau of Alcohol, Tobacco, and Firearms (ATF), or the Energy Department's National Laboratories. This may suggest that increasing awareness or accessibility of these information sources could benefit local law enforcement agencies.

It should be noted that the number of departments that reported receiving assistance from any source (in these areas) represented only a fraction of responding departments; on average only a third of departments requested outside support on any given topic. For example, in video enhancement and analysis, only 28 percent of departments reported receiving assistance from any source. As a result, although only 6 percent of departments reported obtaining that support from the NLECTC, it does represent more than 20 percent of those departments that reported receiving aid in that area.

We also note that, despite the relatively low percentage of departments reporting they received technology support from the NLECTC system, as shown in Tables 25 and 26, the NLECTCs responded to 6,437 requests for assistance in calendar year (CY) 2000. This assistance included answering technical questions, providing technical publications, conducting equipment compliance testing, conducting technology demonstrations, building capacity through specialized technical education, and providing science and engineering advice and support. This level of support has continued into the first six weeks of 2001 with 814 requests from 49 states, the District of Columbia, and Puerto Rico (Caplan, 2001). Appendix B gives specific examples of NLECTC engineering advice and support accomplishments.

PARTNERING FOR TECHNOLOGY-RELATED SUPPORT

In addition to seeking sources of advice, law enforcement organizations can also seek technology information through the formation of alliances or partnerships with other organizations or institutions. As the technological complexity of almost all endeavors has increased over time, such partnership approaches have become very popular among large categories of organizations as a route to keep up with the changing demands of their markets or operational spheres. The RAND Police Survey found that 25 percent of local police are partnering with other local organizations for technology training or support. Rural and small urban less than 25,000 people are less likely than other departments to partner or contract with other organizations for such training or support. The type of organizations that local police have partnerships with range from four-year and community colleges to other law enforcement or government agencies to the private sector (local firms, contractors, etc.). No single type of organization is dominant. The larger the local department, the more likely it is to partner (or contract) with either community colleges, private vendors or contractors, or other government agencies for technology training and support. Private vendors or contractors were the most common type of organization police departments in large urban areas (greater than 225,000) partnered (or contracted) with. These departments also were more likely than any other type of department to partner or contract with trade schools (LETS, 12).

Chapter Eight

RESEARCH, DEVELOPMENT, AND DEPLOYMENT

In this chapter we discuss a number of different activities undertaken by the federal government aimed at helping to meet the technology needs of local and state law enforcement. These activities seek to address the technology adoption roadblocks discussed throughout this report to facilitate the deployment and effective use of new technologies by law enforcement organizations. Though there is some overlap in the particular roadblocks which the programs described in this chapter and those in the following chapter address, those included here are aimed at the barriers of cost, technology risk, and, indirectly, at the unanticipated risks of acquiring new technologies.

Government strategies seeking to neutralize the barriers of cost associated with new technologies include the *direct supply* of materiel to local law enforcement by federal sources (such as the FBI-supplied DrugFire system for firearms analysis) or *direct funding* of purchases by providing money designated for technology to the organizations. These programs, by providing technology itself or earmarked funds, circumvent issues of opportunity cost or trade-offs between technology purchases and investments in other resources.[1] Similar effects can be obtained by providing local law enforcement organizations *access* to federally owned technologies—such as FBI fingerprint data. Providing access to federal technology and directly supplying technologies themselves may also reduce other adoption risks as well. By

[1]It should be noted, however, that circumventing these trade-offs may not be ideal from an overall welfare perspective. If a local police force could better use resources in other ways, requiring that they are invested in technology may not result in the greatest increase in public safety for a given cost.

providing already "validated" and broadly accepted technologies, these routes can limit the technology risk to the local department and the risk of adverse public reaction as well.

Federal programs also seek to provide local law enforcement with *technology evaluation and standards* resulting from the performance of impartial and comprehensive tests on relevant technologies. Such testing, by generating a body of trusted information, can reduce the technical risk associated with procuring a new technology. In addition, the validation of the technology inherent in "passing" federal tests can also make its use more acceptable to public constituencies. Federal *research and development* programs, because of both their information gathering and their legitimating effect on the technologies they examine, could also reduce technical and unanticipated risk. Unlike technology evaluation, R&D also has the potential to affect the absolute and relative costs of technologies as well. By improving existing technologies, R&D or commercialization activities may result in decreasing costs or increasing capabilities. This shift can result in a technology becoming more attractive for deployment over the long term. In addition, R&D activities are the *only* approaches to these technology adoption problems that have the potential to produce entirely new technologies—and perhaps unprecedented capabilities—that could change the entire stage on which law enforcement organizations make technical decisions both in the short and long terms.

It should be noted, in the more detailed findings presented in this chapter, we focus on local departments and forensic laboratories, while not providing data on state police. This is because we believe there were too few responses from state police to the RAND survey for us to assess how well federal programs serve their needs.

Major findings in this chapter include:

- While very few local police departments consider themselves participants in federal R&D or commercialization programs, of those that are their judgment of them is generally positive. The lack of awareness of the nature and benefits of these programs represents an important area of potential improvement to increase the impact and effectiveness of federal efforts.

- Unsurprisingly, members of local law enforcement strongly support programs that send federal resources or technology to local organizations. It is possible, however, that these sorts of short-term approaches to technology problems that address only a limited number of the potential barriers to technology adoption are not the most effective use of limited federal resources.
- Given the importance ascribed to federal standard setting and technology evaluation activities by focus group members and interviewees, the low level of reported utilization of these resources by local law enforcement is surprising. This may represent an important area to address in making these resources more accessible and targeted to satisfy the needs of these organizations.

R&D AND COMMERCIALIZATION

The National Institute of Justice and other federal agencies support efforts to improve technology through research, development, and commercialization. At the time of writing, NIJ's research and development programs and projects, managed under its Office of Science and Technology, include the following:

Officer Protection/Crime Prevention Program: Body Cavity Screening System, Concealable Body Armor, Electromagnetic Portal for Concealed Weapons Detection, Handheld Acoustic System for Concealed Weapons Detection, Handheld Wide-Band Radar for Concealed Weapons Detection, Handheld Ultrasound Through the Wall Surveillance, High-Speed Pursuit Task Force, Low-Cost, Uncooled Thermal Imagers to Enhance Law Enforcement Operations, Millimeter Wave/Infrared Concealed Weapons Detector, Passive Millimeter Wave Camera for Concealed Weapons Detection, Scientific and Engineering Advice and Support for Perimeter Intrusion Detection, Smart Gun, Surveillance/Intrusion Detection Capabilities Enhancements, Technology Introduction: Thermal Imaging and Other Specialized, and Through-the-Wall Imaging Radar.

Less-Than-Lethal Technologies: Capture Net, Laser Dazzler™, Pepper Spray Projectile/Disperser, Ring Airfoil Projectile, Sticky

Shocker, and Test Article Support to Vehicle Stopping Technology Program.

Investigative and Forensic Sciences: DNA Human-Identity Testing Using Time-of-Flight Mass Spectrometry, Rapid DNA Identification Using Microchip-Based Genetic Detectors, Rapid Immobilized Probe Assay for Detection of Mitochondrial DNA Variation, and Tele-Forensics (Crime Scene).

Information Technologies: BORTAC Communications "PATCH," Computer System Development Using Federal Excess Property, Cost-Effective Decisions for Disposal of Police Patrol Vehicles, Dispatcher Activated Response Identification Light (DARIL), Information System Vulnerability, InfoTech Program, Integrated Law Enforcement Face-Identification System (ILEFIS), In-Vehicle Voice Verification (IVVVS), McLean County Communications Study, Metropolitan Nashville Police Department's Palmtop Project, School Safety: The Virtual Private Network, Technical Information Dissemination to U.S. Border Agencies, Telemedicine Demonstration Project, Texas State-Wide Communications Interoperability Study: Scientific and Engineering Advice and Support to Sheriffs' Association of Texas, and Voice Stress Analysis Technology Evaluation.

Counter-terrorism Technologies: Bomb Containment Device, Bomb Technician Data Retrieval Tool, Bomb Technician Training Tool, Center for Civil Force Protection, Chemical/Biological Equipment Guidelines, Explosive Diagnostics, First Responder Quick-Escape Mask, Flying Plate Disrupters, Improved Bomb Robots, Light-Weight Chem-Bio EOD Suit Testing, Mass Transit Protection Sensor Technology, Personal Alarm Monitor, Radar-Based Through-the-Wall Surveillance System, Radar Flashlight, Standards Development, and Threat Assessment.

Technology Tools for Training and Simulation: Bomb Threat Training Simulator and Weapons Team Engagement Trainer.[2]

In addition to R&D to devise new technologies that are not currently available, there is also significant federal activity in technology

---

[2] See http://www.nlectc.org.

commercialization. Commercialization involves adapting technology already developed for other applications (such as military use) to address the needs of law enforcement. Such activities are necessary for technologies that, while applicable to the law enforcement market, may not have sufficiently large demand to justify private firms investing in the costs of commercialization. The NIJ Office of Law Enforcement and Technology Commercialization (OLECTC), part of the NLECTC system, was created to assist with commercialization, including technology transfer and adaptation of appropriate technology produced in both large and small, private and government organizations.

As is the case for most R&D activities and "behind-the-scenes" product development, the final customers who purchase the resulting products are often unaware of what went into them. Consequently, it is not surprising that only about 20 percent of the departments responding to the RAND Law Enforcement Technology Survey were aware of having received any federal support in the area of R&D or commercialization (Figure 3).[3] Since most local departments do not perform R&D or generally request technology commercialization aid, there is little reason for them to be aware of these programs. As discussed in the earlier sections, the focus of many burdened departments and laboratories is necessarily short term on the immediate priorities of today; as a result, the long-term focus of R&D must seem distant from their current needs.

Restricting attention for the moment to the departments that were aware of receiving aid in this area (see Figure 3), more than 50 percent of that subset (9 percent of all departments versus 8 percent) found the aid at least somewhat helpful (LETS, 13j). As a result, while definitely indicating substantial opportunities for improvement in this area, the programs are perceived as net beneficial even among a population with little reason to be cognizant of them. Examining the data for forensic labs, an audience more likely to be cognizant of R&D, an even clearer majority found federal R&D assistance at least somewhat helpful (FTS, 18j).

---

[3]For the LETS survey to local police, percentages have been statistically adjusted to represent the entire population. See Appendix A for a description of the adjustment methodology. For the LETS survey to state police and the FTS survey to crime labs, results are reported as unadjusted percentages.

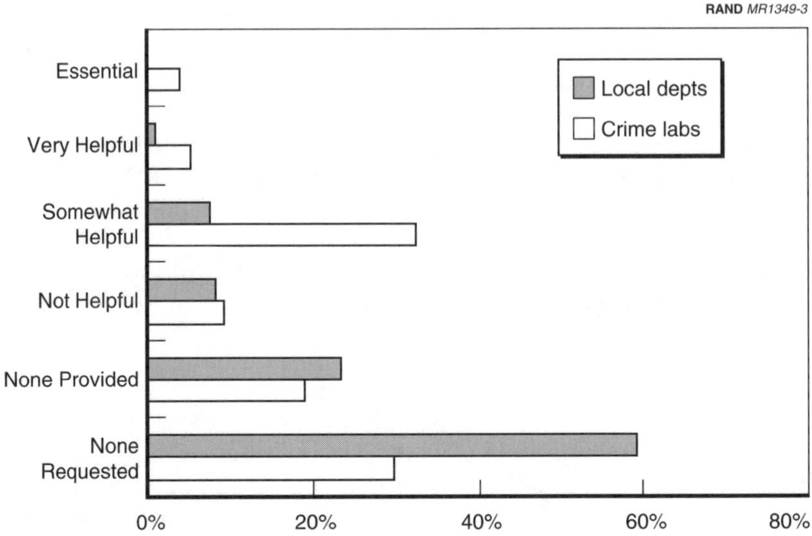

SOURCE: RAND LETS, 13; FTS, 18j. FTS numbers shown are percent of respondents; LETS values are statistically adjusted percentage.

Figure 3—Utilization and Helpfulness of Federal R&D or Technology Commercialization

Although local departments may not rate the importance of federal R&D, standards development, or commercialization as highly as direct funding, this should not be interpreted as "evidence against" the support of these activities. There is a real need for federal sponsorship in these areas because the law enforcement market is neither big enough nor lucrative enough to attract sufficient private sector R&D investment.

TECHNOLOGY DEPLOYMENT

Given the legitimate interest in attracting funding to support their departments and agencies, it is not surprising that state and local law enforcement agencies like federal support in the form of funding for technology acquisition. As alluded to in the opening of this chapter, such federal aid need not be traded-off against other potential uses of resources. Furthermore, if it has been earmarked for specific technologies or devices, then the funds need not even be traded-off among different technology options. Such an approach can represent a legitimate *short-run* approach to law enforcement technology shortfalls. The more fundamental question that must be answered is whether funding for technology acquisition is the most effective and efficient way to allocate limited federal resources, especially over the long term. While a direct funding or supply strategy does decrease shortages quickly, once the funds are spent the investment can only depreciate as the purchased technologies age. Alternatives such as R&D (discussed above), providing access rather than ownership, provision of information (including testing, evaluation, and standards), and leadership in coordinating multi-jurisdictional use of technology could be better in the long term.

Direct Funding

Given the institutional requirements required to participate in federal programs or request grant money, it is not surprising that larger local departments received more funding for technology acquisition. While only 36 percent of rural departments reported receiving such support during the past year, 40 percent of urban departments serving populations less than 25,000, 71 percent of departments serving 25,000–75,000, 75 percent of those serving 75,000–225,000, and 79 percent of departments serving populations larger than 225,000 received funding for technology acquisition (LETS, 13a; FTS, 18a).

The success rates for departments—the percentage of organizations that reported receiving requested federal funding in this area—are also quite dependent on department size. While only 3 percent of the largest urban departments reported not receiving federal aid which they requested, this number increases up to a maximum of 41 percent for rural departments.

Among local departments, a large majority of those receiving federal funding for technology characterized it as at least somewhat helpful (Figure 4). Of the total survey sample, 29 percent of local police departments characterized such support as very helpful or essential. Among responding forensic laboratories, 46 percent rated such support similarly.

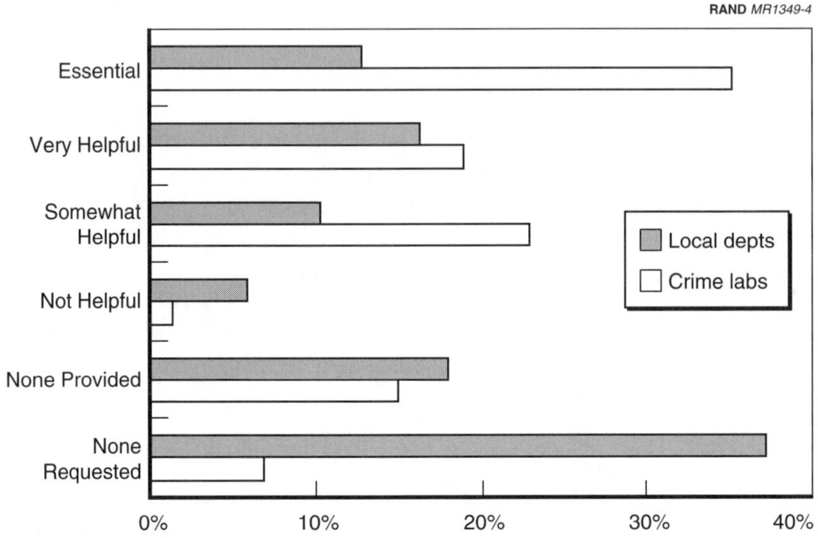

SOURCE: LETS, 13a; FTS, 18a. Numbers are percent of agencies responding as indicated to the question, "During the past year, to what extent has federal support in [this area] been helpful to your agency in carrying out its mission?" FTS numbers shown are percent of respondents; LETS values are statistically adjusted percentages.

Figure 4—Utilization and Helpfulness of Federal Funding for Technology Acquisition

It should be noted that, although the disproportionate representation of larger departments in this area could be related to their size, because many of these departments police areas of much higher crime than small rural departments, there may be sound reasons for the concentration of resources.

Direct Supply

In addition to providing funding, some federal programs provide technology directly to police departments or crime labs. For both laboratories and departments a large majority of those aware of receiving federal technology rated it as at least somewhat helpful (LETS, 13b; FTS, 18b). Among local departments 29 percent characterized federally supplied technology received during the past year as very helpful or essential. Among forensic laboratories 43 percent rated such support similarly (Figure 5).

Access

Rather than providing technology to local departments, another strategy involves providing access to federal technology. By centralizing a common resource, this strategy can reduce costs and make it easier to keep the relevant technology "up-to-date." Among local departments, 13 percent (Figure 6) characterized access to federal technology received during the past year as very helpful or essential. Among forensic laboratories 43 percent rated such support similarly (LETS, 13c; FTS, 18c).

RAND *MR1349-5*

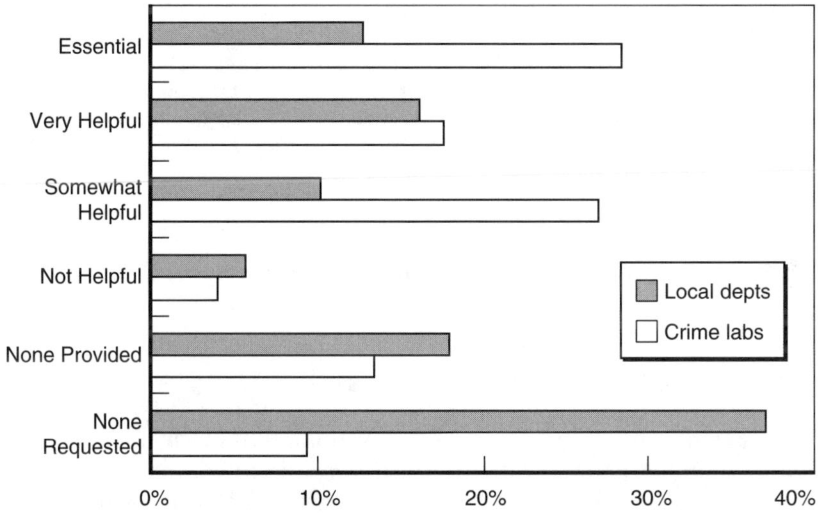

SOURCE: LETS, 13b; FTS, 18b. Numbers are percent of agencies responding as indicated to the question, "During the past year, to what extent has federal support in [this area] been helpful to your agency in carrying out its mission?" FTS numbers shown are percent of respondents; LETS values are statistically adjusted percentages.

Figure 5—Utilization and Helpfulness of Direct Supply of Federal Technology

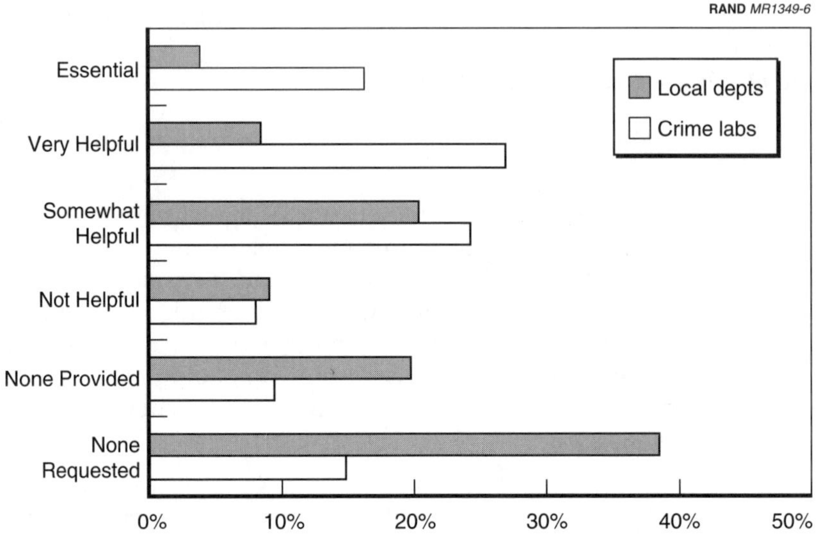

SOURCE: LETS, 13c; FTS, 18c. Numbers are percent of agencies responding as indicated to the question, "During the past year, to what extent has federal support in [this area] been helpful to your agency in carrying out its mission?" FTS numbers shown are percent of respondents; LETS values are statistically adjusted percentages.

Figure 6—Utilization and Helpfulness of Federal Access to Technology

Testing, Evaluation, and Standards

Because of the range of technology options that are available to organizations, it is often difficult or impossible to gather and analyze enough information on each product and make an informed decision. This can be especially problematic for organizations, like law enforcement, that are under short-term time and performance constraints. As a result, impartial and rigorous technology evaluation can be a great help to these organizations by gathering, analyzing, and presenting data on various technology choices to make it possible to rapidly chose among them.

Although the federal government is not in a position to rate competing products or technologies the way the Consumer's Union does in its publication *Consumer Reports*, it can establish performance standards and, in some cases, identify which products meet those standards (see Table 27). A noteworthy example is the work by the National Institute of Justice (NIJ) and the National Institute of Standards and Technology (NIST) Office of Law Enforcement Standards (OLES) in establishing standards for personal body armor and conducting a voluntary body armor compliance testing program.[4]

Akin to standards are "best practices." Examples of this include *Best Practices for Seizing Electronic Evidence,* jointly prepared by the International Association of Chiefs of Police and the U.S. Secret Service, and *Crime Scene Investigation: A Guide for Law Enforcement,* published by the National Institute of Justice. In some instances where it is not clear what are best practices, it is possible to say what are bad practices, that is, what *not* to do.

The RAND survey found that 45 percent of all local police departments with more than 100 officers, but only 26 percent of departments with fewer officers, reported having received federally supplied information on technology evaluation or standards during the past year.

Table 27

Equipment Testing Program

Testing and Evaluation	No. tested in 1999	No. passed in 1999	No. tested in 2000	No. passed in 2000
Body Armor (Ballistic and Stab)	183	132	340	198
Pistol Testing	23	17	—	—
Handcuffs	2	—	2	—
Patrol Vehicles	10	—	12	—
Vehicle Tires	3	—	—	—
Vehicle Brake Pads	—	—	28	—
Protective Gloves	—	—	27	—

[4]For more information, see http://www.nlectc.org/National/bodyarmor.html.

As was the case for R&D previously, when the views of the subset of respondents who were aware of receiving federal aid in this area were examined, the overall impression is generally positive. Seventy-one percent of local police departments responding to the RAND Law Enforcement survey reported either not requesting or not receiving any federal assistance in the form of technology evaluation or standards during the year. Forty-two percent of respondents to the RAND Forensics Technology survey reported not requesting or not receiving federal assistance of this type (Figure 7). This apparent lack of utilization of federal standards setting and technology evaluation services is in marked contrast to the support of these activities expressed by participants in RAND focus groups. As one focus group participant put it, "without federal support for technology standards and commercialization, the law enforcement community is destined to continue to be disappointed by vendors who try to sell them secondhand technology originally designed for other purposes."

Of the 27 percent of the local police departments that reported they received federal assistance in the form of technology evaluation or standards, two-thirds evaluated the assistance as being at least somewhat helpful. Few regarded this assistance as essential. Among the 58 percent of crime labs that reported they received this type of assistance, almost seven-eights found the assistance at least somewhat helpful. About one in five of those respondents viewed the assistance as either very helpful or essential (LETS, 13f; FTS, 18f).

Coordination

There are many ongoing efforts involving federal agencies and others to coordinate, harmonize, or standardize data, procedures, or technologies. XML (the Extensible Markup Language) was briefly mentioned earlier; it is but one of a number of transnational, national, and regional efforts that is likely to yield substantial improvements in ability of agencies and other groups to share information and solve interoperability problems.

The Justice Department's Information Technology Initiative is coordinating all activities associated with integration of justice information systems at the state and local levels. Such coordination efforts

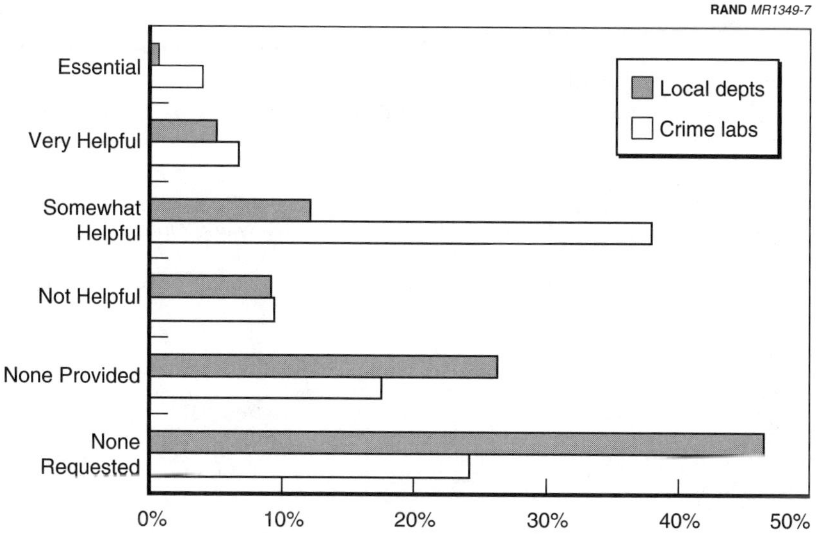

SOURCE: LETS, 13f; FTS, 18f. Numbers shown are percent of respondents. FTS numbers shown are percent of respondents; LETS values are statistically adjusted percentages.

Figure 7—Utilization and Helpfulness of Federal Technology Evaluation or Standards

are immensely complex. For example, besides having to specify compatible formats and using compatible technology, data sharing has to take privacy concerns into account. The U.S. Department of Justice, Office of Justice Programs, working with the Office of the Ontario Information and Privacy Commissioner, has drafted a set of privacy design principles for an integrated justice system.[5] These include: purpose specification, collection limitation, data quality, use limitation, security safeguards, openness, individual participation, and accountability. Each of these principles is, in itself, fairly complex.

---

[5]See http://www.ojp.usdog.gov/integratedjusticepdpapril.htm for a working paper dated April 5, 2000.

We noted above that the RAND survey found a low rate of linkage of files among agencies and other jurisdictions. As obstacles to sharing information are removed or reduced, state and local agencies will not automatically know how to exploit the new possibilities.[6]

---

[6]For a more comprehensive description of the current infrastructure for justice information sharing, see the Global Justice Information Network, *Annual Report 2000,* which is accessible at http://www.iir.com/global/report.htm.

Chapter Nine

TECHNOLOGY APPLICATION

After provision of information and the development and/or deployment of a commercialized technology, the final step of the technology adoption process for an organization is applying the technology to its operational problems. Because such a process is learning intensive and often difficult, providing application assistance can often aid in removing barriers to effective use of technology. Because of the difficulties that can occur, a number of government strategies exist to attempt to facilitate complete technology adoption so law enforcement organizations are able to use their acquired technologies to the greatest public benefit. The strategies discussed in this chapter focus mainly on the human factors associated with technology adoption though, through the provision of information, they can also serve to reduce some of the other risks as well.

The forms of technology support discussed in this chapter include *technology assistance*, such as science or engineering advice and support and *technology advice*, which focuses on selection of technologies and is disseminated through publications or web sites.[1] Both of these mechanisms, by trying to convey lessons about technology adoption or support acquisition, help members of these organizations more effectively learn what they need to put new technology to effective use. By providing broader technical information, they may also reduce the technological risks and make it easier to

[1]An example of such technology advice, which is of particular interest to smaller departments is the Spring 2000 issue of International Association of Chiefs of Police, *Big Ideas for Smaller Police Departments*, "Acquisition of New Technology: A Best Practices Guide."

discern the relative costs and benefits of technologies as well. *Technology news*, conveyed through federal reports, newsletters, and other channels has similar impacts. Support of local law enforcement personnel attending *technology conferences* is a route more completely aimed at the human factors of technology adoption. Similarly support of *training programs*, by providing the opportunity to directly teach officers or staff what they need to know to get the most out of technology, can also be beneficial in this area.

Key Findings from this chapter include:

- The fraction of departments receiving various types of federal technology application assistance vary markedly both among program types and, within individual programs, with department size. While trends do not always favor the largest departments, they never favor the smallest.
- Although the majority of recipients for all technology assistance programs at least find the aid somewhat helpful, it is clear that opportunities exist to improve the support that is provided. In addition, the relatively low percentages of departments that report receiving assistance suggest an opportunity to promote and broaden the programs to a wider audience if resources are available to do so.
- For all programs, survey respondents from forensics science labs are uniformly more enthusiastic and positive about the benefits and effectiveness of these programs. This suggests that current mechanisms connect with and serve this audience better than analogous programs for the broader law enforcement community.

It should be noted that, as was the case in Chapter 8, the findings presented in this chapter focus on local departments and forensic laboratories, while not providing data on state police. This is because we believe there were too few responses from state police to the RAND survey for us to assess how well federal programs serve their needs.

TECHNOLOGY ASSISTANCE

Through its technology assistance programs the National Institute of Justice (NIJ), the Federal Bureau of Investigation (FBI), and other federal agencies bring technology and specialized expertise to bear on local criminal investigations. Such assistance includes audio enhancement of tape recordings, still photo enhancement of surveillance videotapes, analysis of computer files, and metallurgical evidence analysis. In addition to contributing to the investigations in which the analyzed evidence plays a part, such assistance can also transmit information about novel technological possibilities and techniques.

The RAND survey found that 40 percent of local police departments with more than 100 officers, but only 19 percent of departments with fewer officers, reported having received federal technology assistance, such as science or engineering advice or support, during the past year.[2] Although success rates for departments—the percentage of departments that actually received aid that they requested—did vary by size, it did not follow a smooth pattern (Table 28).

Among local departments that expressed an opinion on received federal technology assistance, a large majority found it at least somewhat helpful (LETS, 13g; FTS, 18g). Opportunities for improvement

Table 28

Percent of Local Police Receiving Requested Federal Technology Assistance During Past Year, by Population Served

	Rural	Urban <25K	Urban 25–75K	Urban 75–225K	Large Urban >225K
Technology assistance	32%	35%	47%	77%	53%

SOURCE: LETS, 13g. Numbers are statistically adjusted percent of local police in each size strata indicating federal support requested in the past year was provided. Weighted n=8,170.

[2]For the LETS survey to local police, percentages have been statistically adjusted to represent the entire population. See Appendix A for a description of the adjustment methodology. For the LETS survey to state police and the FTS survey to crime labs, results are reported as unadjusted percentages.

are suggested in the large fraction of departments that reported not receiving or requesting any assistance and the fact that so few of the departments that found the aid helpful found it "very helpful" or "essential." The respondents to the Forensics Technology Survey indicate that a much larger fraction of the surveyed laboratories had requested and received aid than had police departments. Of those receiving it, a very large majority indicated that it was at least somewhat helpful and approximately 16 percent of the survey respondents indicated it was very helpful or essential (Figure 8). Additional information on the specific sources of technology assistance utilized by local law enforcement and criminal laboratories for specific purposes is available in the companion volume to this study (Davis, Schwabe, and Fricker, 2001).

In conducting this study, we learned of several notable achievements of NLECTCs in providing technology assistance to local police agencies, such as the work in Utica, New York, to improve arson investigation and in Ventura, California, to design an information systems and communication infrastructure. It should be noted that the problem with advertising such success stories, which would certainly increase awareness and demand for these services, is that the increase could potentially exceed the capacity of the NLECTCs to supply technology assistance.

NEWS

The provision of news about new technology through federal reports and newsletters is another way to support technology adoption efforts at the state and local level. The RAND survey found that 57 percent of all local police departments with more than 100 officers, but only 41 percent of departments with fewer officers, reported having received news about technology from federal agencies during the past year. Unlike previous programs, the highest success rates—departments in fact receiving technology news which they requested—were observed for medium-sized departments (25,000–75,000 and 75,000–225,000 citizens).

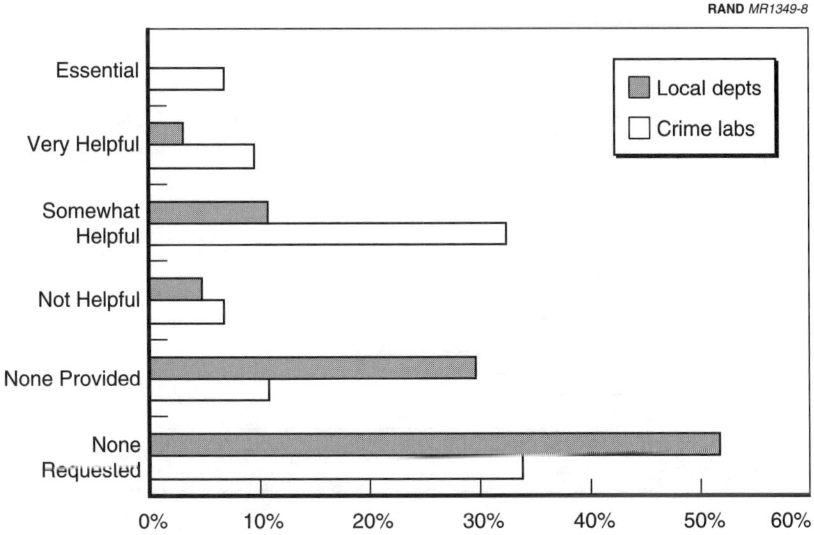

SOURCE: RAND LETS, 13g; FTS, 18g. FTS numbers shown are percent of respondents; LETS values are statistically adjusted percentages.

Figure 8—Utilization and Helpfulness of Federal Technology Assistance

Among laboratories and departments that expressed an opinion on received technology news, a large majority found it at least somewhat helpful (Figure 9). A smaller number of the respondents indicated that news was either very helpful or essential. This, in contribution with the number of laboratories and departments that did not request or receive federal technology news, represent important areas for program promotion and improvement.

In an effort to improve the provision of such technology knowledge, the Office of Justice Programs (OJP) has been exploring additional options and distribution routes. From several conferences and focus groups, the OJP has identified a strong desire among state and local agencies for establishment of a Web-oriented resource center, which would include a staff available to answer questions and help direct people to other sources of information. Efforts are under way to identify what the content of a resource center should be.

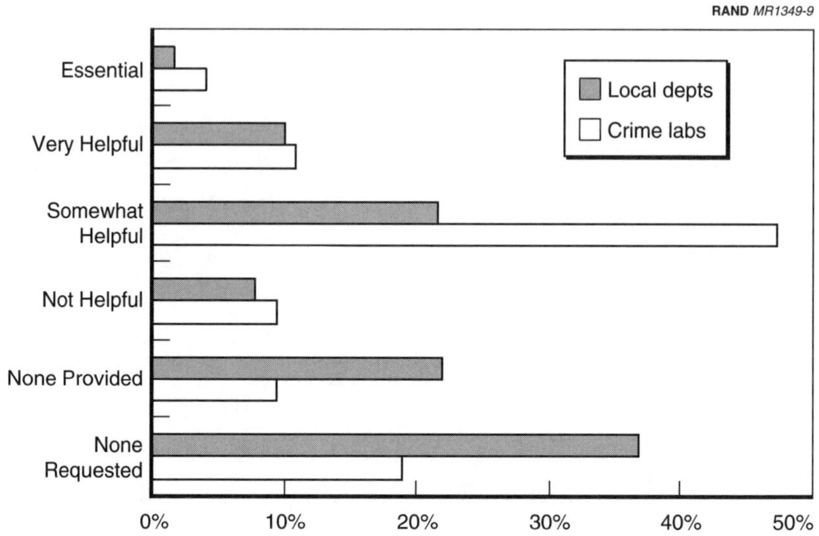

SOURCE: LETS, 13e; FTS, 18e. Numbers shown are percent of respondents. FTS numbers shown are percent of respondents; LETS values are statistically adjusted percentages.

Figure 9—Utilization and Helpfulness of Technology News from Federal Agencies

ADVICE

One potential aid federal agencies can provide to police departments and laboratories is advice on technology selection and procurement. The RAND survey found that 38 percent of all local police departments with more than 100 officers, but only 25 percent of departments with fewer officers, reported having received advice from federal agencies on selecting technology during the past year. Department success rates in receiving requested technology advice also varied by size (Table 29).

Among local departments expressing an opinion on received technology advice (Figure 10), a modest majority believed that it was at least somewhat helpful (approximately 14 percent of respondents

Table 29

Percent of Local Police Receiving Requested Advice from Federal Agencies on Selecting Technology During Past Year, by Population Served

	Rural	Urban <25K	Urban 25–75K	Urban 75–225K	Large Urban >225K
Advice on selecting technology	45%	44%	67%	71%	58%

SOURCE: LETS, 13d. Numbers are statistically adjusted percent of local police in each size strata indicating federal support requested in the past year was provided. Weighted n=8,170.

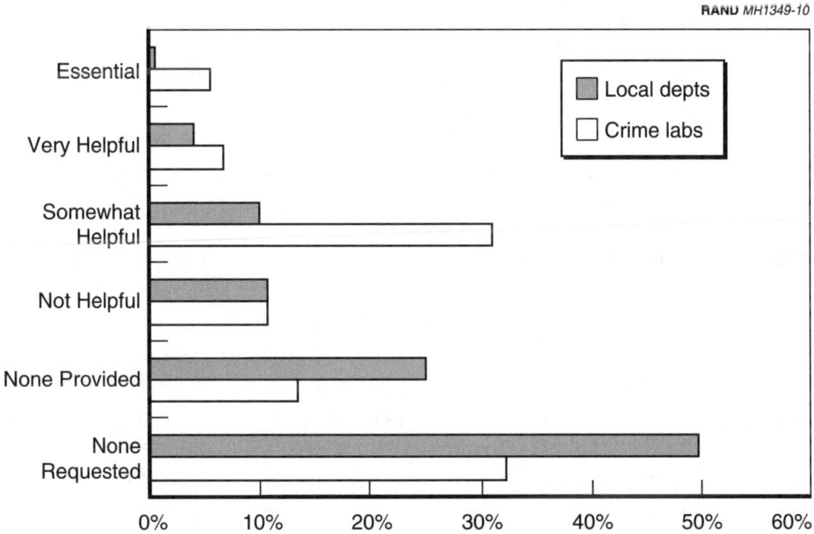

SOURCE: LETS, 13d; FTS, 18d. FTS numbers shown are percent of respondents; LETS values are statistically adjusted percentages.

Figure 10—Utilization and Helpfulness of Federal Advice on Selecting Technology

believed the advice was somewhat helpful or very helpful versus 10 percent of respondents who believed it was unhelpful); for forensic laboratories, a much larger fraction found the advice at least somewhat helpful and a much larger fraction of laboratories found the advice either very helpful or essential than was reported by police departments. As was the case for previous programs, it is clear that more police departments and laboratories could benefit from federal technology advice if more was requested or provided. In addition, the relative opinion of the support received in this area suggests this might be an opportune target to better match the advice provided to the needs of its recipients, especially local police departments.

CONFERENCES

Conferences, by allowing access to the most up-to-date technology and training opportunities, can provide an important source for technical information and knowledge. Eighteen percent of rural police departments reported receiving technology-related conference support from federal sources during the past year. Percentages were higher for urban departments serving up to 75,000 (24–31 percent) and larger urban populations (42–45 percent) (LETS, 13b).

Examining how respondents characterized the conference support, the difference between police departments and crime laboratories is striking (Figure 11). First, in the case of the laboratories, a large majority of the respondents indicated they had received federal assistance in this area; of those, a very significant majority found the support at least somewhat helpful (by a factor of 20 to 1 over those that found it unhelpful). A majority of respondents (51 percent) rated the support as very helpful or essential. This suggests that conference support may be a very effective and certainly desired mechanism for supporting forensic laboratories. In contrast, many fewer police departments responding to the survey indicated that they had received such support and, among those that had, their judgment was far less positive. Those finding the support at least somewhat helpful still outweighed those who found it unhelpful by three to one, however.

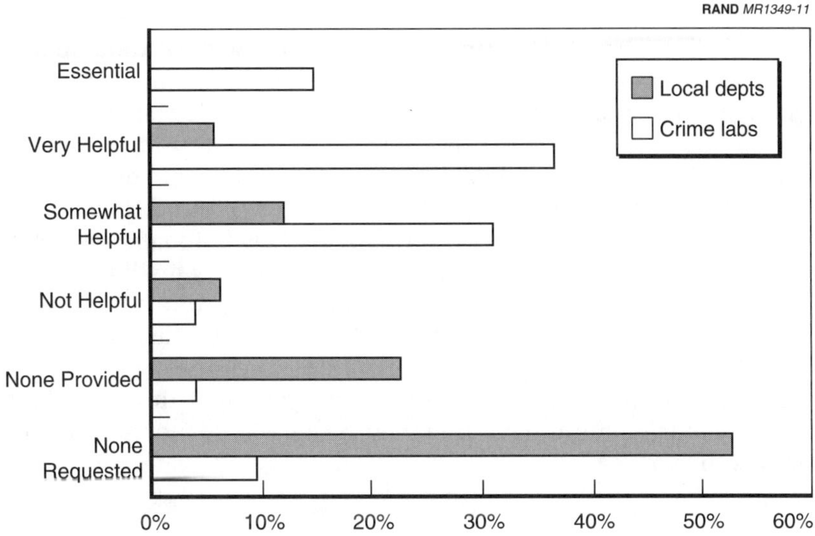

SOURCE: LETS, 13i; FTS, 18i. FTS numbers shown are percent of respondents; LETS values are statistically adjusted percentages.

Figure 11—Utilization and Helpfulness of Federal Technology-Related Conferences

TRAINING

From the discussions previously about the importance of training to adopting new technologies and the perceived shortages of training resources and technology, it is clear that technology training is an important area for federal attention. The RAND survey found that 35 percent of local police departments with more than 100 officers but only 20 percent of departments with fewer officers reported having received federal support in the form of technology-related training during the past year. The success rates of obtaining requested training were also higher for larger departments with 56 percent of departments with more than 100 officers reporting that they received requested training in comparison to only 42 percent of smaller departments.

Just as was the case for conference support, the responses of crime laboratories to the RAND survey were far more positive about federal technology training than those from police departments (Figure 12). A very large majority of crime laboratories reported receiving federal technology training and, of those, labs that found it at least somewhat useful outweighed those that did not by more than 25 to 1. Almost half the total respondents (49 percent) found the training very helpful or essential. Many fewer of the Law Enforcement survey respondents reported receiving training, and those who did were less positive. In the case of local police departments, those finding the training at least somewhat helpful outweighed those that did not by only 2.4 to 1. This suggests opportunities for improving both the accessibility and awareness of these training opportunities to local police departments and crafting their content to be more responsive to their needs.

RAND *MR1349-12*

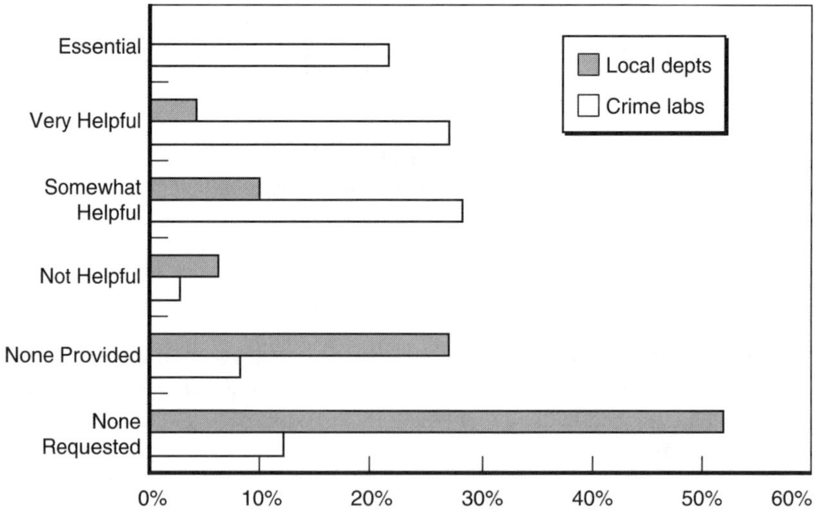

SOURCE: LETS, 13h; FTS, 18h. FTS numbers shown are percent of respondents; LETS values are statistically adjusted percentages.

Figure 12—Utilization and Helpfulness of Federal Technology-Related Training

Chapter Ten

CHALLENGES AND CHOICES

The job of law enforcement is never an easy one. Operating within a complex society, police organizations must be constantly on the lookout for new threats to public safety and devise ways to counter those threats. Those who endeavor to break the law are constantly adopting new forms of technology. Recent years have shown not just the appearance of crimes that would have been unheard of two decades ago, including identity theft and cybercrime, but also the effects of the most raw and basic technology adoption by criminals. It is difficult to envision a more dramatic demonstration of the technological threat to law enforcement organizations than a shoot-out where police are outgunned by individuals wielding automatic weapons protected by body armor superior to that available to the officers standing against them. The stakes involved in facilitating the adoption of new technologies can, obviously, be very high.

In an age of concern about the responsible use of public funds, however, technology can also play a role in making law enforcement more efficient and effective with the ability to accomplish more with fewer resources. These technologies—via their contributions to management of operations or allocation of officers—can potentially allow society to gain a desired level of public safety at a more reasonable cost. Because of technology's potential to both increase the effectiveness of police forces in the face of evolving crime and allow more effective police operations, society as a whole has an interest in understanding and, if need be, facilitating technology adoption by state and local law enforcement organizations.

NUMERICAL LESSONS FROM THE SURVEYS

One of the main goals of the RAND Law Enforcement Technology Survey was to identify what technologies were and were not available to law enforcement organizations around the country and to gauge their future technology needs. As a result, the results of the survey could be summarized on a basic level by simply delineating the range of technologies that are generally not available to local police departments. These were technologies that, when asked about their current accessibility and any barriers to their acquisition, respondents indicated were not currently available and were not "unnecessary" (LETS, 22, 25–29). As a result, this represents a list of potentially needed technologies. The listing of the technologies, along with the percentage of local police departments lacking them, is included in Table 30. The table is sorted in order of decreasing non-availability, down to a cutoff of 25 percent. It should be borne in mind that because the surveys did not cover every current or potential law enforcement technology, this represents a limited slice of the technologies which are and are not available to local police departments.

When examining such a summary listing of unavailable technologies, it is important to place the survey responses in an appropriate context. Although the values included above are the percentages of law enforcement that indicated these technologies were both unavailable and not unnecessary, it is highly likely that there is a significant barrier for a survey respondent (especially for a survey of this kind) to designate a technology as unnecessary.[1] For example, it is the case that more than two-thirds of local police departments lack "necessary" radioactive agent detection equipment (Table 30). The degree of necessity of this technology might be appropriately calibrated by considering the net increase in public safety that might accrue from providing each of these departments a Geiger counter compared to providing training equipment to the 28 percent of respondents who lacked it (or upgrading the training equip-

[1]There is a legitimate personal and organizational interest not to refuse any resources that might improve law enforcement performance even marginally. As a result, while it is unlikely that a circumspect observer would assert that each of the 57 percent of local departments that lack night vision capability truly "need" it, there is also a clear rationale why many survey respondents would indicate that they did.

Table 30

Technologies Not Available to Local Police

Technology	Not Available	Technology	Not Available
Detection and analysis of cyber-attacks	79%	Computers in patrol cars	58%
Blister/nerve agent protective clothing	79%	Electronic listening	57%
Video conferencing equipment	75%	Night vision devices	57%
Kinetic energy projectiles	75%	Vehicles—special purpose	45%
Chemical agent detection	71%	Crowd or riot control	44%
Long-range video monitoring	69%	Computer-based training	41%
Stun devices/projectiles	68%	Conference call equipment	36%
Radioactive agent detection	66%	Computer assisted dis-patching (CAD)	35%
Explosives detection	64%	Integrated data bases	34%
Polygraph equipment	64%	Protective gloves, helmets, and shields	34%
Fleeing vehicle interdiction equipment	63%	Audio-visual equipment to obtain evidence	30%
Concealed weapon detection devices	62%	Training equipment	28%
Bomb containment/ disablement equipment	60%		

SOURCE: LETS, 22, 25–29. Numbers are statistically adjusted percent of local departments reporting technology is not available.

ment of the many respondents who indicated that theirs was insufficient). All technology acquisition decisions, whether they are made at a local or national level, are a calculus of trade-offs and it is important to remain cognizant that there are serious consequences of losing sight of that fact.

In addition to identifying technologies that are unavailable to state and local police organizations, the RAND surveys also asked for information on the age and quality of currently available technologies. By identifying their current technologies as either obsolete or "old but serviceable," survey respondents provided a list of technologies

Table 31

Technologies in Need of Replacement by Local Police

Technology	Obsolete	Old but Serviceable	Either Obsolete or Old
Radio equipment	10%	46%	56%
Training equipment	10%	35%	44%
Administrative/accounting systems	18%	26%	44%
Computers in workspaces	7%	34%	41%
Audio-visual equipment to obtain evidence	12%	28%	40%
Crowd or riot control	12%	25%	37%
Protective gloves, helmets, and shields	9%	25%	34%
Ballistic- and stab-resistant armor	8%	25%	33%
Computer-based training	9%	20%	29%
Integrated data bases	8%	22%	29%
Conference call equipment	3%	24%	27%
Vehicles—special purpose	4%	21%	25%
Cellular telephones	2%	24%	25%

SOURCE: LETS, 22, 25–29. Numbers are statistically adjusted percent of local departments reporting as indicated.

that many be candidates for replacement in near to medium term. These responses are included in Table 31 in decreasing order of the fraction of departments characterizing them as "Obsolete" or "Old but Serviceable," down to a cutoff of 25 percent (LETS, 22, 25–29).

From the perspective of the policymaker, several things stand out from such a numerical summary of the survey results. Most striking is the fact that 18 percent—almost one in five local police departments—indicated that their administrative or accounting systems were obsolete; without such input from departments it would be difficult to see that such an "unglamorous" technology might indeed be a high priority for local police forces. Other entries on this table are less surprising. The appearance of computers and cellular telephones is not unexpected given the short product cycles and rapid obsolescence of those products. The appearance of ballistic-resistant armor (stab-resistant armor is not broadly available) on the list also holds a relevant lesson from the perspective of law enforcement technology policymaking. While bulletproof vests do "age" and become worn over time, studies have shown that the protective properties of the armor do not break down.[2] As a result, the notion of an "obsolete" bulletproof vest is a complex one likely based more on the obvious importance of the technology (and its performance) to officers rather than the technology itself.

Just as was the case in examining the summary list of unavailable technologies above, the importance of reasoned trade-offs among technologies must remain firmly in mind. Although a third of departments report that their workspace computers are "old but serviceable" the costs and benefits of upgrading them all to "state of the art" must be weighed against the unavailable technologies above, providing training to better use technologies that are already available, or performing R&D to generate the potential that superior technologies will be available in the future.

CONCEPTUAL LESSONS FROM THE SURVEYS

Just as the aggregate survey results suggest the trade-offs that must be made at the highest levels of technology decisionmaking, they also emphasize the trade-offs and other obstacles that face technology adoption at the micro level. Returning to the general framework presented in the introduction, the results of the surveys indicate that, for law enforcement organizations, each of the four obstacles to technology adoption must be considered. For the broad classes of technologies included in the survey, respondents identified all four:

- Costs
- Technology Risk
- Human Associated Risks
- Unanticipated Potential Costs

Of the reasons cited by respondents, cost routinely stood out as the primary obstacle to the adoption of new technologies. Such a result is not unexpected given that, at some price point, any technology be-

[2]See "Old Armor Tests As Good As New," http://www.nlectc.org/.

comes attractive for purchase and, until it reaches that level, cost does stand as an obvious initial obstacle to using the technology. If cost is a sufficient obstacle, none of the other barriers to adoption are relevant; if you don't have the opportunity to adopt a technology because the cost is too high, how well you adopt it is not an issue. The fact that many respondents cited cost, however, likely also represents the important and difficult trade-offs that must be made within police departments. Because of the labor intensity of their activities, technology acquisition must always compete with "placing more police on the street" or paying overtime to extend an investigators work on a pending case. In addition, because of the variety of ways police departments could allocate their funds, trade-offs among technologies are also likely very important. It is not just the cost of the technology that dictates its desirability but the perceived benefits that are associated with purchase. In this light it is not surprising that fewer large urban departments cited cost for some technologies that are particularly suited to solving the problems of an urban police force.

But just as cost is clearly a barrier, other barriers to adoption are important as well. Departments are concerned about the technical risks associated with some technologies as expressed by their indicating that the "reliability/effectiveness" of the technology could be a barrier to acquisition. Smart guns stand out as such a technology where, if police departments are to adopt the technology, steps must be taken to develop it to the point that these concerns are satisfied. The human factors associated with technology adoption, as emphasized in concerns about training, training technology, and other sources of information are also clearly important for both law enforcement agencies and forensic science laboratories. The barrier that finding sufficient trained personnel poses to the effectiveness of forensic science laboratories stands as a troubling but important finding of this study. Currently, most law enforcement organizations' technology adoption efforts are less affected by concerns with unanticipated effects like public opinion. Important exceptions exist to this trend, however, including stand off and direct electrical devices, once again emphasizing the differences that exist among technologies with respect to adoption barriers.

LOWERING THE BARRIERS TO TECHNOLOGY ADOPTION

Because of society's interest in law enforcement adopting technologies which make its activities more effective, promote public safety, and advance the cause of justice, how policies can be crafted and targeted to reduce barriers to adoption is of clear interest. As discussed in Chapters 7–10, it is clear that federal programs designed to lower these barriers, whether through R&D, provision of technical information, support of training, and other activities are making progress in making the acquisition process easier for law enforcement organizations. The relatively modest percentages of particularly local law enforcement departments that are currently being reached by these programs suggests that they have the potential to more broadly serve the needs of the nation's police, provided sufficient organizational and financial resources are available. It would be counterproductive to encourage more police forces in the country to take advantage of these resources if the increase in demand would overwhelm the system and make it less effective for everyone. On the other hand, while the generally positive views of federal support programs on the part of those departments that have benefited from them are encouraging, the low intensity of these views suggests that there is more that can be done to increase the relevance of the aid and advice and craft it to better serve the needs of local police. The generally much more positive views of federal programs by the crime laboratory respondents to the survey is noteworthy suggesting that these programs are more effectively reaching their intended audience.

Policy Considerations

When considering federal responses to these issues, it is important to consider policies not just in terms of short-run effects but also how their long-term effects can be crafted for the social good. The programs that were viewed most positively by respondents to these surveys—direct provision of technology and transfer of federal monies to the local level for technology purchases—are uniquely short-run strategies. Although it is understandable why law enforcement practitioners, who are primarily asked to solve problems in the short term, would find the quick effects of these types of programs appealing, they may not be the best way of investing limited federal resources. Provision of money that is designated for technology support also eliminates the trade-offs that must be made at the local level among competing potential uses for the resources; when a particular technology is mandated as a condition of support, even trade-offs among technologies may be eliminated.[3] While providing a technology to a police force today will generate immediate benefit (assuming that the other barriers to adoption of the technology are surpassed), its return will gradually decrease over time as the system is worn out or becomes obsolete. It is possible that other programs, whose returns increase with time rather than decrease, might be better policy targets.

One example of such an increasing returns target is the provision of technical training to help overcome human barriers to technology adoption. Training of individuals has the possibility to not just improve how individuals use today's technology but improve their use of technologies in the future; the potential for trained individuals to spread their knowledge within their organizations provides the chance for increased returns on the investment even in the short term. The RAND survey results and findings from interviews strongly suggest the need for increased training, including training to use technology already available or being procured. This particular topic was brought up with respect to small rural departments all the way up to a large urban department with a billion dollar budget. Respondents spoke of considerable, wasteful redundancy in training curricula. Training technology is developing rapidly on many fronts, including law enforcement. Distance learning and interactive computerized training offer promise for overcoming at least some of the obstacles (e.g., lack of time and money) agencies face in training their personnel.

Like training, R&D can also address the technology adoption barriers of organizations, but it is a much more long-term strategy. It is only though research that new technological possibilities are discovered and current technologies are adapted and applied to the needs of law enforcement. Because of the unique characteristics of the law en-

[3]It should be noted that these effects have the potential to generate significant distortion in the way that funds are used at the local level since it is the competition among different potential uses and the trade-offs among alternatives that could lead to more efficient allocation.

forcement technology market, private firms may ignore roles in this area not taken by the public sector. The importance of research as an enabling approach to these problems—exemplified by the important advances in body armor and other technologies which outfit today's officers—point out that, even though local forces may not see immediate benefits and, as a result, may not be as supportive of these programs, they are important nonetheless. Research and development can also take as a goal not only developing new technologies but improving those which are already available; selecting a target of providing rapid, cost-effective DNA analysis capabilities could go a long way toward removing the backlogs and staff shortages that currently prevent forensic laboratories from making their full potential contribution to law enforcement. Research and development therefore likely represents a unique role for government to support work that not only lowers adoption barriers for current technologies but attempts to apply novel technologies to other needs of law enforcement as well.

OVERARCHING TECHNOLOGY CHALLENGES

Another place where federal involvement can play a very important role in the technology challenges of law enforcement is by facilitating or spearheading the type of "large scale" technical changes that can only come from the upper levels of a social system. One example of such a role is systems integration among the many different government activities that have an effect on law enforcement agencies. Although taking an integrated view toward crime control as involving more than law enforcement seems sensible to many people, it requires at least two technical changes:

> First, as we find the need to integrate criminal justice and social services databases, we will need to work through confidentiality requirements. Second, optimal analysis would allow us to commingle an individual's data from various disciplines. This will be problematic because all data systems have difficulty in positively identifying and tracking individuals. The problems of individual identification will increase significantly as we try to join databases (O'Connell, 1998, p. 95).

> That is the big challenge before us at the dawn of the twenty-first century: to embark on the unification of our technology with our humanity (Dertouzos, p. 314).

One person we spoke with described broad integration concerns and challenges as follows:

> As we're looking at integration issues throughout the country, the general focus that we're driving towards is not only criminal justice but *justice*. We're looking into expanding the civil aspects as well as the criminal and [asking] what are the juvenile, family court, and domestic relations issues. [You can draw the boundary around law enforcement] but that's not where most of the thinking has gone these days when we're talking about integration and flow of information.
>
> What we're seeing more and more often is that the CIOs [Chief Information Officers], if they're powerful people and if they're very directly connected to the governors, are playing this role of defining the infrastructure, the standards, and the architectures that should be used for the sharing of information. They are right at the centerpiece of the design of the integrated criminal justice information systems. That's as it should be, because there is a growing recognition among probably more of the urban or more sophisticated sheriffs and police chiefs that there is a need to flow information in and out of the criminal justice system with transportation, education, social services, and the other non-criminal justice entities that plug into [a Unified Criminal Justice Information System] from both the front end and the back end.

The Office of Justice Programs and its Bureau of Justice Assistance of the Department of Justice have been working in partnership with SEARCH, the National Consortium for Justice Information and Statistics, to better define both "the system" and "integration."[4] The Justice Department's Office of Justice Programs has also funded the National Association of State Information Resource Executives

---

[4]See SEARCH Special Report, "Integration in the Context of Justice Information Systems: A Common Understanding," Revised April 2000, at http://www.nasire.org/hotIssues/justice/SEARCHintegdef.pdf.

(NASIRE) to develop architectures and standards for sharing information.[5]

CONCLUDING THOUGHTS

Although recent crime rates have been at low levels, preliminary figures show some increases in 2000. As one response to this change, federal officials may choose to increase technology-related support to state and local law enforcement agencies. Although the primary motivation for this may be desire to increase public safety (through reducing crime), the goals of improving law enforcement efficiency (reducing costs over the long run) and promoting justice (while reducing incidence of injustice) can and should also be taken into account.

Historically, "cops on the street" and hardware have had much more political appeal than "softer" technologies. Respondents to the RAND surveys are crying out for training and software support, for increased ability to access and share data, and for forensic capacity to prevent and to solve more crimes. Police leadership—especially in the larger jurisdictions—sees the need for technology to support accountability.

Progress in some of these areas is just a matter of funding—and distributing funds where they are most needed. In other areas, such as data sharing, there are both technical and legal obstacles to realizing full potential. For example, agencies have legitimate concerns about ensuring security and integrity of data they share; recipients of data need assurance that it is accurate and current. Laws may need to be revised, to allow data sharing, where appropriate, while safeguarding legitimate privacy concerns.

In some areas, progress can be made simply by "doing business" differently. For example, if agencies within or among jurisdictions were able to form buying consortia to purchase technology, substantial unit cost reductions could be achieved. To do this, however, consortia members have to consider individual agency purchasing systems

---

[5]See NASIRE Report, "National Information Architecture: Toward National Sharing of Governmental Information," at http://www.nasire.org/hotIssues/justice/Fullrept.pdf.

and provide ways to access the pool without violating purchasing agreements. This is, of course, much easier said than done, given the desire of local government to maintain local control.

It is becoming increasingly evident that a systems approach to public safety, cost reduction, and justice is the most appropriate way to pursue each of these goals. Concentrating solely on one aspect, such as public safety/crime reduction, leads almost invariably to imbalances and undesirable side effects. For example, concentrating only on apprehending, convicting, and incarcerating criminals leads to prison costs that are not sustainable in the long run and the perception of injustice among groups disproportionately incarcerated.

Inherent in a systems approach is the need to look beyond narrowly defined law enforcement. We have done that in this study by including forensic science and touching on courts, corrections, and schools—as well as by considering training in conjunction with technology and by relating technology and accountability. But there are many aspects of the systems approach that can be dealt with adequately only in the context of specific locales and situations—and that is beyond the purview of this study.

Strategies for promoting the diffusion of worthwhile technology deserve careful consideration. Differences among technologies, as suggested by the survey results, are very important. Diffusion of simple technology, such as collapsible batons replacing older types, probably don't require more than vendors' marketing strategies and natural word-of-mouth communication among police. Other technologies, such as AFIS, NCIC, or the futuristic lab-on-a-chip or lab-in-a-box, will most likely require more holistic diffusion strategies, including training and interagency protocol development, to overcome the considerable barriers that exist to the adoption and effective deployment of any new and powerful technology.

Recommendations

In light of the information contained in the RAND surveys and the discussions surrounding it, it is relevant to ask how the discussion contained here can contribute to the construction of a reasonable, forward-looking federal technology strategy to support state and local law enforcement. To that end, we suggest the following points:

- To avoid wasteful spending and to ensure technology is used to good effect, we recommend that federal initiatives providing technology hardware or software include provisions for training. It appears that all too often procurements are made under the false assumption that "somebody else" will take care of training.
- To help law enforcement agencies make more effective and less disappointing technology acquisition decisions, we recommend continuing and publicizing federal testing, evaluation, and standards setting for technologies needed by state and local agencies.
- To enhance public safety, we recommend providing data network access to all police and sheriffs' departments that have unmet needs for it. No American community—large or small—wants its officers to lack information that could have been available to recognize and apprehend dangerous criminals wanted in other jurisdictions.
- To meet the demands of investigation as well as prosecution, we recommend building forensic capability well beyond current levels. This could include providing screening-test technology to first responders, as well as increasing training, recruiting, and retaining forensic scientists. We recommend it include increased federal support of R&D of forensic science techniques and technologies. One possible focus of this R&D might be on lowering the acquisition cost for a standard, known throughput capability suite of forensic laboratory equipment.
- To correct evident competitive disadvantages of smaller law enforcement agencies, we recommend that federal agencies make a serious effort to make it easier for rural and small urban police and sheriffs' departments with real, unmet needs, to obtain funding and other technology-related support. Although some rural and small departments may have crime rates too low to warrant more substantial investment in modern technology, other rural or small departments suffer unmet needs because they lack political clout or skilled personnel available to write grand proposals.
- As a cost-effective investment, we recommend increased federal funding of R&D of technologies that automate or otherwise increase productivity of what are presently labor-intensive or

training-intensive processes. Such technology can help make high quality law enforcement more affordable.

- To promote police accountability and to provide more objective evidence of lawbreaking, we recommend that all or most patrol cars be equipped with video cameras and wireless networked computers. Videotaping provides objective evidence useful for suspect identification and prosecution, as well as for resolving complaints of police misconduct. Rapid access to current data on stolen vehicles, outstanding warrants, etc., can reduce officer uncertainty in confrontational situations. The most practical federal role in this may be in defining or developing equipment suites or standards, rather than in directly funding their acquisition.
- To reduce confrontational uncertainty, risk of injury to officers and the public, as well as risk of confrontations escalating into civil disturbances or abuse of police power, we recommend continued federal support for the development, testing, and deployment of technology that can be carried in patrol cars or on officers to detect concealed weapons at a safe distance. We note that military and other security forces have similar needs.[6]

These technology-specific goals, if coupled with attention to the technology adoption considerations discussed here, could lead to more effective use of technology by law enforcement organizations nationwide which, we believe, has the potential to contribute significantly to public safety, long-run cost reduction, and justice.

---

[6]It is also important to note that there are significant applications for any nonportable versions of this technology that might be produced during development of patrol car or police officer models. For example, stationary devices that could detect the presence of concealed weapons could be placed in schools and airports detecting the "arrival" of any weapons into a monitored area. Such technology, if it was made reliable and cost effective enough, could allow educational institutions in particular to devote less of their resources to security and more to the primary goal of student instruction.

Appendix A

RAND SURVEY METHODOLOGY

Two surveys were fielded: a Police Survey of state, county, and city police departments, and a Forensics Survey of state and local (city or county) crime laboratories. The surveys were distributed via a combination of random, systematic, and convenience sampling schemes (depending on the type of agency). The Police Survey was distributed via a stratified random sample to municipal police departments, a simple random sampling scheme to state highway patrols and state police departments, and via a systematic sample of tribal police departments.

As part of the municipal police department sampling, specific cities, and some agencies surrounding those cities making up a metropolitan network of law enforcement response capabilities, were forced into the sample (i.e., they were sampled with certainty). These specific cities are special in some way, either because of their size or technology needs or in terms of the types of law enforcement problems these agencies encounter, so sampling them with certainty ensured they were included in the sample. The Forensics Survey used convenience sampling, via wide distribution on the Internet.

THE SAMPLE AND RESPONSE RATES

The sampling frame for the Police Survey was taken from National Public Safety Information Bureau directory data. The sampling frame for the Forensics Survey was taken from the membership listings of ASCLD. A total of 710 surveys were mailed to the various types of police agencies. The number of surveys distributed and returned are discussed further and tabulated in Table 32.

Table 32

Survey Response Rates for Police and Sheriffs' Departments

Type of Organization	Sampling Frame (N)	Sample Drawn (n)	Number of Responses (m)
State	50	17	15
Municipal	15,765	687	411
Tribal	272	6	2
Total:	16,087	710	428

State Police Organizations. Seventeen state police and highway patrol organizations (i.e., highway patrol, state police, etc.) were randomly drawn from each of the 50 states—one organization per state was selected. Of the 17 organizations solicited, 15 responded to the survey, for an 88 percent response rate.

Municipal and Local Police Organizations. We selected 687 organizations to be surveyed; 661 were randomly drawn, and 26 were systematically selected due to their size or because they were of specific interest. Of the 687 departments solicited, 411 responded, for a 60 percent response rate. Details of the stratification scheme are discussed in the next subsection.

Tribal Police. Six tribal police organizations were selected to be surveyed and two responded, resulting in a 33 percent response rate. The organizations were not randomly drawn, so the results are not statistically generalizable to any larger population. Because we only received two surveys we did not include tribal police in the report write-up. However, in general, their responses tended to be similar to those of rural law enforcement agencies.

Details of the Local Police and Sheriffs' Department Stratification

In order to ensure adequate representation among all types of local police and sheriffs' organizations, the organizations were stratified by number of officers in the department (1–30, 31–100, 101–300, and more than 300) and area served (urban or rural) and then randomly drawn within strata. The number of officers was obtained from

National Public Safety Information Bureau directory data[1] and the urban/rural classification was taken from the "Area Resource File." We used the "Rural/Urban Continuum Code," as defined by the Department of Agriculture. The codes form a classification scheme that distinguishes metropolitan counties by size and non-metropolitan counties by degree of urbanization or proximity to metropolitan areas. Counties with codes 7–9 were defined as rural, and all others were defined as urban. Table 33 gives the breakdown by strata.

The rural stratum is largely composed of small departments (96 percent), "small" meaning departments with between one and 30 officers. The remaining four percent (n=146) have departments in the 31–100 officer range, and one rural department falls in the 101–300 range.

Table 33

Survey Response Rates for Local Police

#	Strata	Sampling Frame (N)	Sample Drawn (n)	Number of Responses (m)
1	Rural	3,638	173	74
2	Urban, 1–30 officers	8,824	100	53
3	Urban, 31–100 officers	2,334	125	77
4	Urban, 101–300 officers	685	126	88
5	Urban, 301+ officers	284	163	94
	Total:	15,765	687	386

Note: We ultimately deleted one observation from stratum 2 and one from stratum 5 due to ineligibility.

[1]Two hundred thirty organizations were missing the number of officers. For these, we imputed the number of officers from the county population. To do this, we regressed number of officers on county population size, for those departments not missing either variable, and then we used the resulting regression to predict the number of officers for those records missing this data. Result: We imputed values for 72 municipal and local police organizations and 158 campus police organizations. Of these, 12 were drawn in our sample (10 municipal/local and 2 campus).

Of the total population for each stratum listed above, 26 departments were forced into the sample. One came from stratum 3, seven from stratum 4, and 18 from stratum 5. The organizations forced into the sample are as listed in Table 34.

Table 34

Departments Forced into the Police Survey Sample

State	County	Department	Stratum
AK	Anchorage	Anchorage Police Dept	5
CA	Alameda	Berkeley Police Dept	4
CA	Alameda	Oakland Police Dept	5
CA	Los Angeles	Santa Monica Police Dept	4
CA	Los Angeles	Culver City Police Dept	4
CA	Los Angeles	Los Angeles Police Dept	5
CA	Los Angeles	Los Angeles Co Sheriffs Dept	5
CA	San Francisco	San Francisco Police Dept	5
FL	Dade	Miami Police Dept	5
HI	Honolulu	Honolulu Police Dept	5
IL	Cook	Evanston Police Dept	4
IL	Cook	Chicago Police Dept	5
IL	Cook	Cicero Police Dept	4
MD	Montgomery	Montgomery Co Police Dept	5
NJ	Hudson	Jersey City Police Dept	5
NY	New York	New York City Police Dept	5
NY	Westchester	Yonkers Police Dept	5
NC	Mecklenburg	Charlotte/Mecklenburg Pd	5
PA	Allegheny	Pittsburgh Bureau Of Police	5
SC	Charleston	Charleston Police Dept	5
TN	Davidson	Nashville Metro Police Dept	5
TX	Dallas	Dallas Police Dept	5
TX	Dallas	University Park Police Dept	3
TX	Dallas	Garland Police Dept	4
VA	Arlington	Arlington Co Police Dept	5
VA		Alexandria Police Dept[a]	4

[a]Alexandria, Va., is not in a county.

ANALYTIC WEIGHTS FOR MUNICIPAL POLICE DEPARTMENTS

We developed analytic weights to account for the stratified sampling of municipal departments and for non-response. These statistical adjustments allow the analysis to properly infer back to the overall municipal police department population. The calculations were done as follows:

Municipal departments were randomly sampled within strata. As shown in the next table, a predetermined number of respondents were drawn from strata j, n_j, so we can write

$$\text{P(department } i \text{ in strata } j \text{ is sampled)} = n_j / N_j,$$

where N_j is the total number of municipal police departments in strata j in the sampling frame. In the absence of non-response and ineligibility issues, the weight for department i in strata j would simply be $W_i = N_j / n_j$. However, non-response and ineligibility affect n_j and N_j respectively, and they must be adjusted to arrive at weights which will allow proper inference back to the population of interest.

Non-response is often accounted for using the propensity score method of Little and Rubin (1987) to determine the probability that department i responds given that department i was sampled. This probability is calculated by fitting the logistic regression model

$$\text{P(department } i \text{ responds} \mid \text{department } i \text{ was sampled)} = \frac{\exp(\hat{\beta}_0 + \hat{\beta}_1 X_1 + \ldots + \hat{\beta}_r X_r)}{1 + (\hat{\beta}_0 + \hat{\beta}_1 X_1 + \ldots + \hat{\beta}_r X_r)}$$

where the coefficients are estimated using relevant information that predicts which of the sampled departments responded to the survey and which did not. However, the only covariates available in the sampling frames are the same that were used to define the strata. Thus, we more simply calculated

$$\text{P(department } i \text{ responds} \mid \text{department } i \text{ was sampled)} = m_j / n_j.$$

From this, the probability that department i in strata j was sampled *and* responded, $p_r(i)$=P(department i is sampled and responds), was calculated as

p_r(i) = P(department *i* responds | department *i* was sampled)

% P(department *i* in strata *j* sampled) = $m_j / n_j \% \, n_j / N_j = m_j / N_j$.

As a result, we defined the analytic weights for the municipal police departments as $W_i = N_j / m_j$.

Standard Errors

In all of the statistical calculations, we used the linearization method (Skinner, 1989) as implemented in the SUDAAN software (Shah, Barnwell, and Bieler, 1997) to account for the stratified sample in our estimates of standard errors. The linearization method uses a first order expansion to approximate via a weighted sum of random variables a nonlinear statistic. The variance of the nonlinear statistic is then estimated by the variance of the weighted sum, which is estimated using standard formulas for linear statistics. See Skinner (1989) or Shah et al. (1997) for complete details on this method.

Survey Design Methodology

The Law Enforcement Technology Survey (or "Police Survey") was intended to elicit information on current technology usage and availability, priority ratings with respect to training, technology-related, and computer-related needs, factors that may influence acquisition decisions, quality of technology in current usage, sources of technology-related information and support, and assessment of federal support received within the past year.

The survey used a combination of multiple choice and open-ended questions. The draft survey instrument was pilot tested by local law enforcement officers, NIJ representatives, and reviewed by a psychologist with extensive experience in survey design as well as by RAND's Survey Research Group. Based on feedback from these individuals, the survey was modified and finalized.

This questionnaire was designed to be a mail survey with both telephone and mail follow-up. The survey was initially fielded the first week of June, with survey packets addressed and mailed to the head of each law enforcement agency in our sample. While the packet was addressed to the head of each agency, it was understood that in most cases it would be distributed to the person (or persons) within that agency primarily responsible for the organization's technology-related needs, or to those best able to answer questions regarding the survey's content. Therefore, chiefs were asked to fill out and return a self-addressed postcard indicating which officer within their agency would be the contact for the survey. This information allowed RAND's Survey Research Group to follow-up directly with the individual officer tasked to complete the survey within each agency. The instrument was designed to be completed in about 20 minutes.

Because this population is one that has been "over-surveyed" (e.g., a number of agencies commented that on average they receive as many as 5–6 surveys/day), we utilized intensive telephone follow-up done in two waves in order to maximize the response rate. This strategy included an initial telephone call to non-respondents, combination of faxing and mailing to non-respondents a replacement survey, and telephone follow-up requesting that completed questionnaires be returned to us as soon as possible. This strategy was instrumental in obtaining an overall response rate of 56 percent at the time of the analysis. In fact, over the course of several months additional completed surveys have trickled in increasing the overall response rate to greater than 60 percent.

FORENSICS SURVEY

The RAND Forensics Survey was distributed by e-mail attachment, fax, and web site to 165 public crime laboratories across the United States.[2] The survey was completed by 70 respondents, providing data on 105 laboratories in 27 states.[3] Sixty-three percent of the respondents represented state crime labs, 16 percent municipal crime labs, 11 percent county crime labs, 6 percent other crime labs, and 4 percent coroners or medical examiners (Table 35).

---

[2]This was meant to distribute the survey to the every state and local laboratory whose director is a member of the American Society of Crime Laboratory Directors (ASCLD).

[3]Several state agency respondents provided data on their multiple-laboratory crime lab system.

Table 35

Agencies Responding to Forensics Survey

State	Number of Responses	Number of Laboratories	State Crime Lab	County Crime Lab	Municipal Crime Lab	Coroner/ Medical Examiner	Regional /Other Lab
AR	1	1	1				
AZ	2	2			2		
CA	18	18	14	3	1		
CO	1	1	1				
DE	1	1	1				
FL	5	12	10	2			
GA	1	7	7				
HI	1	1			1		
IA	1	1	1				
ID	1	1	1				
IL	6	6	6				
IN	2	5	4				1
LA	1	1					1
MA	1	1			1		
MD	3	6	4	2			
ME	1	1					1
MI	2	2	2				
MN	2	4	3		1		
MO	3	8	6		1		1
NC	2	2	1		1		
NE	2	2	1		1		
NH	1	1	1				
NJ	2	5	4	1			
NV	1	1					1
NY	5	5	3	1		1	
OH	3	3			1	1	1
OK	1	1			1		
PA	1	1		1			
TN	1	1	1				
TX	3	14	13			1	
VT	1	1	1				
WI	1	3	3				
WV	1	1	1				
Total	78	120	90	10	11	3	6

Appendix B

EXAMPLES OF NLECTC TECHNOLOGY ASSISTANCE ACTIVITIES

This compilation of noteworthy NLECTC accomplishments was provided by Congressman Sherwood Boehlert's office.

Utica (NY) Arson Strike Force

In 1997, the City of Utica was experiencing an arson rate that was twice the national average and three times the state average. Worse, arson cases were being cleared at a rate well below the national average. NIJ, working with the U.S. Fire Administration, was able to help local police and firefighters deploy new tools. Those efforts involved galvanizing the community, as well as employing technology, and they produced impressive results. Such success offers an instructive example of what NIJ's National Law Enforcement and Corrections Technology Center system can do. Leveraging the multi-billion dollar taxpayer investment in the U.S. Air Force Laboratory in Rome, New York, the NLECTC was able to create affordable technology tools for the task force's use. In less than a year, the arson rate had been cut in half, the clearance rate was among the best in the nation, many arrests had been made, and the conviction rate stood at 100 percent.

Sullivan County (NY) District Attorney Child Torture/ Murder Case

Sullivan County District Attorney Stephen Lungen requested that NLECTC-NE provide technology assistance in the case of a 3-year-old child who was tortured and murdered. By providing photo enhancements to the District Attorney, the prosecution was able to prove that the child was intentionally tortured before being killed. Using advanced computer technology, NLECTC-NE staff scanned autopsy photographs of the victim's injuries; methodically removed the wounds and manipulated the photographs to look like natural, uninjured skin; and then placed the injuries back into the photographs to illustrate the process in which they had been inflicted. Using these photo enhancements, the DA was able to demonstrate systematic and intentional torture before the child was killed, an aggravating factor under New York State's first degree-murder statute. After the defense attorneys viewed the presentation, the defendants pleaded guilty to first-degree murder in exchange for life in prison without the possibility of parole.

Wasilla (AK) Police Department Receives Thermal Imager

The Border Research and Technology Center helped the Wasilla, Alaska Police Department obtain a state-of-the-art thermal imager by leveraging a $79 million investment made by the U.S. Army Night Vision and Electronic Sensors Directorate and the Defense Advanced Research Projects Agency. In addition to providing the department with the ability to operate at night, they are evaluating the device to determine how well it works in extremely cold climates.

New York County (NY) District Attorney's Office, Security Fraud

The New York County District Attorney's Office requested that NLECTC-NE provide technology assistance in a high-profile security fraud case involving the analysis of 23 videotapes after the FBI indicated its case backlog (six months per tape) would prohibit a timely investigation. NLECTC-NE also assists the FBI with audio/video analyses to relieve the Bureau's backlog and improve its ability to meet field agents' time constraints.

Central New York Law Enforcement Network Demonstration

NLECTC-NE is working with several law enforcement agencies in central New York to enhance their information technology capabilities. Specifically, they are assisting in developing a network that will allow the Utica Police Department, Oneida County Sheriff's Department, and Madison County Sheriff's Department to share mug shot records.

Office of the Attorney General Medicaid Fraud Control Unit (NY)

An undercover investigation by the Office of the Attorney General Medicaid Fraud Control Unit yielded numerous taped conversations between informants and a suspect that were very unclear and virtually useless as evidence. NLECTC-NE provided the technology needed to filter out enough background noise so that the tapes could be used against the suspect. As a direct result of NLECTC-NE audio analysis efforts, the target was arrested and arraigned in Bronx County, New York.

Pomona (CA) Police Department, Child Pornography Case

Center staff assisted in analyzing evidence in a child pornography case for the Pomona Police Department. After recovering a large number of images from the suspect's computer, investigators realized that a large effort would be required to open and review each image to determine its relevance to the case. Center staff developed a mechanism to create thumbnail versions of each image that could be browsed using Netscape or Internet Explorer. Investigators now have a tool to examine many images quickly and open only those that appear to be relevant to their case.

Los Angeles County (CA) District Attorney's Office, Homicide Investigation

An investigator from the District Attorney's Office asked whether the audio forensics staff at NLECTC-West could perform astronomy calculations to establish the time of death in a homicide case for which they were already performing audio enhancements. To refute the suspect's claims, the DA's investigators needed to know the time at which the moon set at a specific location on the Angeles Crest Highway on a certain date in 1999. Center staff provided the calculated time of moon set and a graph of the moon's location together with the skyline to the DA's Office. This technique can likely place the time of death within a few minutes, with the largest error actually being the accuracy of the suspect's statement.

Alhambra (CA) Police Department, Embezzlement Case

NLECTC-West assisted the Alhambra Police Department on a computer case that involved finding documents in connection with an embezzlement scheme. The suspect, an accountant, had filed false papers naming himself as the sole owner of corporations that his clients were incorporating. The clients discovered that the accountant had named himself the owner of their companies. The investigator requested help in identifying files from the suspect's computer that might demonstrate his procedures. NLECTC-West staff improved the search programs to help identify files that contained greater numbers of target phrases. Center staff were able to recover evidence of the false filings, and the case is proceeding toward trial.

Los Angeles (CA) Police Department, Homicide Investigation

NLECTC-West is assisting the Los Angeles Police Department (LAPD) Crime Laboratory with a forensic investigation. The case involves the nondestructive analysis of a fractured sear (cocking piece) from a Walther PPK handgun used in a shooting fatality. The lab has asked the Center to determine the functional condition of the sear immediately following the shooting. The primary objective of this study is to assess whether a light impact from a plastic mallet (an analysis action taken by the crime lab during investigation) could provide sufficient impact energy to fracture the sear. Additionally, the Center is assessing the likelihood that the sear could have been broken as a result of the pistol being dropped onto a carpeted floor at the time of the shooting. The Center is now analyzing further questions posed by the District Attorney's Office.

Whittier (CA) Police Department, Child Kidnapping and Molestation

Whittier police investigators requested assistance from NLECTC-West in viewing videotapes in a child kidnapping and molestation case. A young girl was picked up by a white male in his thirties, who brought the child to several stores, where he bought presents to gain her confidence; brought her to his apartment, where he molested her; and then returned her to the neighborhood in which he had originally found her. Although the child could not describe the suspect very well, she did remember where they went shopping. Videotapes were gathered from the store surveillance systems, but they had been recorded in various modes and speeds that made it difficult for the detectives to examine all of them carefully in a controlled manner. The Center was asked to assist investigators' efforts to view all of the tapes. Several images showed a young girl walking hand in hand with a white male. The Center enhanced the images of the young girl, and detectives confirmed she was the victim. Center staff then found frames that showed the suspect in the best possible light and enhanced the frames. The detectives took color prints from the Center and met with the squad investigating sexual predators, who identified the suspect and provided an address for the Whittier detectives. The suspect confessed to the molestation and is in jail.

Los Angeles (CA) Police Department, Bombing Investigation

In May 2000, the Los Angeles District Attorney's Office began prosecution of a bomb defendant who had been arrested after an explosion occurred inside his residence. The LAPD bomb squad had discovered substantial damage to the defendant's apartment and to the apartment below. Unexploded devices found inside a closet were destroyed as a result of safety concerns. NLECTC-West experts were able to identify chemical components in the bomb residue and initial chemical components used to create the destructive devices. They used computer printouts obtained by the LAPD bomb squad to correlate the explosive potential of the chemicals with the actual destruction caused by the explosion. In addition, the experts informed the prosecutor of the technical issues that would arise during the trial and prepared him to understand the ramifications of arguments that would be presented by the defense. The defendant had been previously tried on similar charges and had evaded conviction by claiming the devices were merely fireworks that had exploded. The Center's experts were able to point out the lack of traditional fireworks chemicals in the debris and explained to the jury that this particular chemistry produced explosives and not fireworks. The prosecutor had no other sources of expertise to assist in this case because the bomb squad unit did not possess the type of knowledge required. The defendant was convicted.

Los Angeles County (CA) Sheriff's Department, Homicide

The Los Angeles County Sheriff's Department requested that NLECTC-West provide technology assistance in their investigation of the homicide of a young female cheerleader who had been hired to pose in a sport utility vehicle (SUV) photo spread for an automobile magazine. The photo shoot had been conducted in the desert north of Los Angeles. After the victim did not return, investigators found her body in a shallow grave north of the city. The prime suspect was the photographer who had hired the victim. He admitted that she had died during the photo shoot but stated that it was an accident. He admitted that he buried her body but said it was a panic reaction and argued that she had died from asphyxiation during a consensual sexual encounter. The defendant's relatives provided some partially exposed film that they had found near the burial site, which the defendant claimed he had discarded in a panic. The film was purportedly shot with the victim consenting to partially nude photos in the SUV. The victim's face was not in the photos, but the photos did contain the SUV's interior in the background. Image experts at NLECTC-West were able to demonstrate that the upholstery pattern in the photos did not match the pattern of the vehicle used in the photo shoot. Furthermore, lace patterns of clothing in the discarded photos did not match the pattern of clothing worn by the victim. It was concluded that the discarded photos did not come from the crime scene and involved other people and other vehicles. This evidence, along with other elements, helped to convict the defendant.

Washington County (OR) District Attorney Arson/Murder

In February 1996, a single-family frame house burned to the ground. During the investigation, a woman's remains were found in the debris. Her husband was subsequently arrested and charged with arson and murder. The prosecution contended that the husband had shut off the natural gas (LPG) line to the house, disconnected the flex gas line to the dryer, started a small fire, and turned the gas back on at the LPG tank—thus causing the explosion and fire. The defense contended that the fire started in the car in the attached garage and was caused by a short circuit of the battery cable. Analysis performed by NLECTC-West proved that molten brass covered all threads and penetrated the remains of the galvanized coating on test samples and that brass was not seen on metallurgical cross-sections from the dryer connection. Through this analysis, the prosecution was able to prove that the LPG line to the dryer was not connected at the time of the fire. The suspect was convicted of manslaughter and arson and is serving his sentence.

Manhattan Beach (CA) Police Officer Slaying

The NLECTC-West was asked to assist in the murder investigation of a Manhattan Beach police officer. It was near Christmas and officer Martin Ganz was conducting a ride-along patrol with his nephew in the vehicle. Officer Ganz pulled over a motorist for a routine traffic violation in the vicinity of a shopping mall. Officer Ganz was shot, and subsequently executed by the motorist who sped away. The shooting took place in front of a bank that multiplexed seven cameras from various positions inside and outside the bank onto one tape recorder. The camera that had officer Ganz's vehicle in view did not capture the shooting; however, a portion of the suspect's vehicle was captured in another bank camera. Piecing together three images from three cameras, NLECTC-West was able to create a composite vehicle. Patrons of the mall were requested to bring similar configured cars to the mall several weeks later and these various brands were placed in front of the same cameras that captured the suspect's vehicle. Detailed comparison of headlight spacing, reflections from lighting and shape of fenders and roofs led the investigators to conclude that the suspect was driving a particular vehicle that was somewhat scarce. Later, when the suspect was captured in another state, his vehicle was brought back to Manhattan Beach and put in front of the same cameras as before. It matched the vehicle from the night of the murder and convinced the jury that the suspect had been at the location of the murder at the time of the murder.

California Police Chiefs Association, Technology Database

NLECTC-West is working with the California Police Chiefs Association to build an online database to record technology purchases funded this year under a $75 million program from the California legislature that provided a minimum of $100,000 per agency and up to $4 million for some large agencies. The legislature designated the funds to help agencies acquire technology to upgrade their law enforcement capabilities. The Police Chiefs Association asked the Center to support information collection from its member agencies identifying the types of technology purchased and the amount spent on each technology. The Chiefs will analyze the data and present their findings to the legislature to lobby for a second year of program funding, and they wish to receive this information within one month. Approximately 25 percent of the agencies responded within the first week.

School-Based Virtual Private Network for Bloomington-Normal, Illinois

The Southeast Center continues to fine-tune a Virtual Private Network for School Safety to ensure timely, effective, and secure information sharing. The Southeast Center researched, designed, and installed an e-mail based, protected system for information sharing between police, schools, and courts in the Bloomington-Normal area. Technical issues have been resolved; the current challenge is legally overcoming the reluctance to share information about juveniles.

U.S. Border Patrol/El Paso Sector

The Border Research and Technology Center (BRTC) provided science and engineering support to the U.S. Border Patrol/El Paso Sector to address their concern regarding individuals entering the United States illegally through the city's storm drain system. Deterring this illegal form of entry is key to reducing the quantity of illegal contraband smuggled into the United States. These drains also run under several public buildings, which makes them potential sites for terrorist acts. BRTC conducted site surveys, presented methods for securing the drains, and demonstrated equipment (including a video motion detector and micro-power range grated radar). In addition, estimates for sensors, cameras, and radio frequency link equipment have been made.

Statewide Radio Communications Systems Assistance: Texas, Montana, North Dakota, Nebraska, and Colorado

NLECTC-RM is actively involved with technology assistance, including engineering reviews, of statewide radio communications systems that are being proposed or acquired. States that are currently receiving assistance are Texas, Montana, North Dakota, Nebraska, and Colorado. This assistance involves review of their statewide plan and proposed architecture.

Statewide Communications Network

BRTC and NLECTC-RM are working with the Sheriffs' Association of Texas (SAT) to support its Communications Committee's participation in a statewide legislatively chartered task force to review potential solutions to the problem of communications interoperability. In addition to providing NIJ/NLECTC publications and participating in SAT's annual training conference and other activities, both BRTC and NLECTC-RM are invited to attend regular meetings of the Radio Task Force, evaluate survey forms, and assess technical solutions consistent with the overall NLECTC mission. SAT represents all 254 counties.

San Diego District Attorney's Office; El Paso (TX); U.S. Border Patrol, Technology Demonstrations

BRTC leverages commercial-off-the-shelf (COTS) technology to provide science and engineering support and assistance to the San Diego District Attorney's Office, the El Paso Police Department, and the U.S. Border Patrol/El Paso Sector. To date, this support has improved the capabilities of these agencies in the areas of witness protection, interrogation room monitoring, covert surveillance, and specialized intrusion detection. The basis of these improvements is an "investigators' tools" kit consisting of monitoring equipment initially funded through Department of Housing and Urban Development public housing security improvements. In the case of the El Paso Police Department, this assistance resulted in a "lessons learned" report to NLECTC and enabled that department to explore establishing a crime scene teleforensics capability. This ongoing project will involve other law enforcement agencies along the southwest border in 2001.

Governor's Columbine (CO) Task Force

A NLECTC-RM employee, Gene McGahey, has been nominated as the communications resource person to the Governor's Columbine Task Force. This is a high-level panel addressing every conceivable issue which came out of the Columbine High School Disaster. Because of his expertise, McGahey will provide an invaluable service not only to the State of Colorado but in the area of school safety.

Innovative Technologies for Community Corrections

NLECTC-RM is actively addressing the need for technology information among community corrections officials. The first Innovative Technologies for Community Corrections conference was held in June 2000 in Denver, Colorado. Due to the overwhelming response a second conference is planned for May 2001 in Dallas, Texas. The conference will explore practical applications of technologies currently in use as well as technologies not yet available but on the horizon. Topics to be discussed include: non-invasive drug testing, advances in electronic monitoring, automated reporting systems, crime mapping for community corrections, distance learning, supervising high-tech offenders, using polygraph to manage sex offenders, handheld computers for field use, and management issues in implementing technology.

Understanding Wireless Communications in Public Safety Guidebook

NLECTC-RM created this publication for middle- and upper-level managers who are responsible for funding and/or managing communications at their agencies, but have little or no technical background in wireless technology. The guidebook discusses how to plan and manage a communications project, wireless communications technology and issues, and the operations available in wireless communications technology. This manual was written due to the expressed need of practitioners to have information on wireless communications at a layperson level.

Broomfield (CO) Police Department Obtains Crime Lab Microscope

NLECTC-RM helped the Broomfield, Police Department's Crime Lab to obtain its first microscope. The $6,000 microscope was made available through the Federal Property Program. The microscope has enabled the police department to process evidence quicker because it does not have to be sent out to the Colorado Bureau of Investigations. Analyzing items in-house can allow for faster apprehension of suspects.

Rocky Mountain Region Criminal Justice Internet Resource Class

NLECTC-RM offers the Criminal Justice Resource Class quarterly in an effort to make the Internet a resource for law enforcement and corrections agencies. The class includes information on how to track down information, which search engines could be most effective, tours of numerous agency web sites, and a demonstration of how to access crime statistics and research. The class has been presented to more than 125 criminal justice practitioners in the Rocky Mountain region.

Nebraska Correctional Facility, Drug Detection Assistance

NLECTC-RM received a request from a Nebraska correctional institution that was considering purchasing a drug detection system that utilizes ion-trapping technology. They requested assistance in order to make a more informed purchasing decision. NLECTC-RM provided the institution with information on three major vendors, product information, benchmark evaluations on the systems, and contact information for a recognized expert in the field of drug detection systems.

Washington County (WA) Corrections Department

NLECTC-RM received a request from a county corrections department in Washington which expressed concern over the number of suicides that have occurred in their facilities. Over the last two years, four inmates have committed suicide, three by hanging. To provide information to address their need, NLECTC-RM staff located a comparable county facility in New Jersey that had a successful track record in suicide prevention. The New Jersey staff was contacted and agreed to serve as a resource and share their suicide prevention plans with the Washington agency. To address the specific problem of hanging, contact information for two vendors who specialize in suicide prevention garments and blankets were provided.

University of California–Berkeley Police Department

BRTC responded to an urgent request from the University of California–Berkeley Police Department to provide technical assistance in detecting intrusion into agricultural areas where substantial damage to research projects was occurring. Technology advice and support was provided which improved the capabilities of the police department to protect university experiment areas. Additional assistance was provided to campus law enforcement supporting other research institutions through BRTC's support of a statewide conference on this and related crime prevention problems. BRTC has also met with representatives of the San Diego Sheriff's Office (Agricultural Crime Unit) and the University of California/San Diego campus police to render similar support.

Test Article Support to Vehicle Stopping Technology Program

BRTC is assisting NIJ's vehicle stopping technology program through the identification and acquisition of automobiles and other vehicles necessary to accomplish testing goals. Working through the U.S. Marshals Service, BRTC was able to identify for the transfer of 14 vehicles estimated at a value of $75,000. BRTC also provides assistance by serving on the Pursuit Management Task Force.

South Carolina Law Enforcement Division Develops Computer Evidence Recovery Unit

The NLECTC-SE is assisting the South Carolina Law Enforcement Division in developing a special unit to investigate computer-related crimes. The Center has arranged for visits to the Department of Defense Computer Forensics Laboratory, the FBI and Secret Service Laboratories, and the Illinois State Police. The Center has also met with its technical partners at Oak Ridge National Laboratories, Savannah River Technology Center, and SPAWAR to determine what assistance they may be able to provide.

Greensboro, High Point, and Winston-Salem (NC) Police Departments Introduced to Geographic Profiling

The NLECTC-SE has developed one of the few capabilities in the Unites States for geographic profiling and has recently completed training of personnel and equipment installation in three police departments in Greensboro, High Point, and Winston-Salem for a field test of its effectiveness in combating property crimes that often go unsolved. Additionally, the Center has installed a Virtual Private Network Internet-based regional information sharing system to improve the effectiveness of the technology.

NLECTC-SE Conducts Vulnerability Assessments of Information Management Systems

The NLECTC-SE is conducting assessments of the vulnerability of information management systems for law enforcement and corrections agencies. The Center will prepare a guide that can be used by other agencies concerned with the vulnerability of their information systems.

Federal Property Program

In FY 2000, the Federal Property Program assisted in transferring $256,645,499.70 worth of property reaching more than 13,000 law enforcement agencies, more than 1 million sworn officers, and 504 federal agencies. Equipment transferred included vehicles, aircraft, weapons, protective gear, and clothing.

CFX 2000 Offers 28 Agencies Practical Experience in Computer Forensics

CFX 2000, a digital forensics experiment that applied various tools to conduct a planned attack on a computer system, allowed 28 law enforcement agencies to practice solving simulated computer-related crimes. The Northeast Center identified and secured the participation of federal, state, and local law enforcement investigators, examiners, and prosecutors from the Drug Enforcement Agency (DEA), FBI, U.S. Secret Service, New York State Police, Massachusetts State Police, New Jersey State Police, and Erie County, Onondaga County, and Westchester County, totaling 70 personnel. CFX 2000 was a successful event that enhanced the body of knowledge available on electronic crime at the state and local levels.

Corrections Technology Demonstration at Mock Prison Riot

The Annual Mock Prison Riot held at the Moundsville Penitentiary in West Virginia offers corrections personnel an opportunity to learn firsthand tactics, technology information, and applications in a realistic setting. In 2000, more than 1,300 individuals representing 22 states and two foreign countries participated in this four-day event. A total of 70 technologies were showcased as well; scenarios ranging from cell extraction to hostage negotiations were staged to demonstrate appropriate technologies. Courses offered at the Mock Prison Riot included "How to Handle a Riot" and "Vulnerability Assessments for Prisons."

NLECTC-NE Cyberscience Laboratory

NLECTC-NE established the National Law Enforcement Cyberscience Laboratory to provide technology assistance and support to state and local law enforcement agencies. The program develops government, industry, and academic collaboration to address cybercrime technical issues. The Laboratory hosts training in conjunction with the National CyberCrime Training Partnership; helps to transition forensic tools and technology from their technology partner (the Air Force Research Laboratory/Information Directorate) to state and local agencies; helps enhance criminal justice community awareness of cybercrime issues; and provides technology assistance.

NLECTC-NE Law Enforcement Analysis Facility

NLECTC-NE established the Law Enforcement Analysis Facility (LEAF) to provide unique forensic analysis of audiotapes, videotapes, and computer media and to demonstrate audio/video enhancement technologies to state and local law enforcement agencies. LEAF uses state-of-the-art Air Force–developed technologies. The facility has responded to hundreds of requests from police and prosecutors to help solve a wide range of cases, including murder, arson, robbery, fraud, and rape.

Crime Mapping and Analysis Program Assists Law Enforcement Agencies

The Crime Mapping and Analysis Program (CMAP) provides technology assistance and training to state and local agencies in the areas of crime and intelligence analysis and geographic information systems (GIS). The program is currently offered at NLECTC-RM and SE. Since its inception in June 1998, CMAP has offered 35 classes. To date, 306 law enforcement personnel from 36 states have participated in the program. Many of those agencies have initiated crime-mapping programs as a result of their participation.

Operation America

The render safe bomb technology demonstration (formerly known as Operation Albuquerque and Operation Riverside, and now called Operation America) was held from September 18–21 in San Diego. NLECTC-RM and Sandia National Laboratories sponsored the event, which offered 25 bomb technicians the opportunity to learn about the latest render safe technologies. In previous years, this training activity was an extremely large event, lasting nine days, involving more than 100 participants, and requiring complete coordination of the entire city to carry out bomb threat scenarios. To be more interactive, this year's event was restructured to last five days with three days of classroom instruction and two days of range exhibition. As demonstrated by the overwhelming number of letters received by NIJ/OS&T, the event successfully offered a unique view of rendering safe technology development. Plans for future Operation America events include holding them quarterly in various cities to reach the larger bomb technician community.

Northeast Intern Program Opportunities

The NLECTC-NE e-Crime Intern Program offers a unique opportunity to gain knowledge and hands-on experience in the field of cyberscience in the law enforcement community. This program represents a joint venture between academia and the public and private sectors to provide students with a challenging experience in support of cyberscience developments. Students majoring in computer science from Utica College currently intern at the New York State Crime Lab in Albany, where they practice applying their academic knowledge of cybercrime to practical situations. In return, the laboratory benefits from the constant influx of new ideas while at the same time improving the training of new cybercrime investigators. A similar program already exists at the Connecticut Crime Laboratory, and others may be developed with different agencies in the near future.

National Commercialization Conference

The Office of Law Enforcement Technology Commercialization (OLETC) sponsors the annual National Commercialization Conference, which brings together practitioners, developers, and vendors to examine new and emerging technologies for law enforcement and corrections agencies. Topics discussed during the conference include the application and implementation of new technologies, the implementation of ideas from conceptualization to commercialization, provision of assistance to developers for creating business plans or finding venture capitalists, and licensing agreements.

National Public Safety Telecommunications Council (NPSTC) Support Office

The NPSTC Support Office, established at NLECTC-RM, is a federation of 12 associations and two federal agencies representing public safety. The office is currently located at NLECTC-RM and will facilitate the NPSTC precoordination database for the 700-MHz band, which will store the allotted and pending applications for radio frequencies used by public safety personnel. In addition, the office will incorporate team resources to support council requirements. This project will benefit all of the nation's public safety entities and the Federal Communications Commission, as the precoordination database is needed for effective and efficient delivery of the 2,100+ channels in the 700-MHz band.

Los Angeles Terrorism Early Warning Group (LA TEWG)

NLECTC-West was invited to serve as a team member on the LA TEWG. Group activities require law enforcement, medical, transportation, and communications expertise. The LA TEWG has created a methodology for assessing risk to facilities in the region and has developed a set of folders used to compile threat assessments for each facility. In addition the group has developed techniques for intelligence gathering and analysis. Their procedures were utilized during the Democratic National Convention last summer in Los Angeles. With daily involvement of NLECTC-West, the LA TEWG analyzed the procedures and behaviors of the various groups demonstrating at the convention. Using analysis generated on the first day of the convention, they were able to suggest procedures to minimize the potential risk posed by demonstrators intent on disrupting the convention proceedings. The Center is working with the LA TEWG to abstract best practices and procedures, to be shared with other regions wishing to form similar groups.

REFERENCES

ACLU, "ACLU White Paper Says LAPD Fails Citizen Complaint Process Called for by 1991 Christopher Commission Report," http://www.aclu.org/news/n070996c.html.

Austin, J., and P. Hardyman, "The Use of Early Parole with Electronic Monitoring to Control Prison Crowding: Evaluation of the Oklahoma Department of Corrections Pre-Parole Supervised Release with Electronic Monitoring," unpublished report, Washington, DC: National Institute of Justice, 1991.

Barksdale, James L., "Communications Technology in Dynamic Organizational Communities," in Frances Hesselbein et al. (eds.), The Community of the Future, San Francisco: Josseph-Bass Publishers, 1998, pp. 93–100.

Baumer, T. L., and R. I. Mendelsohn, "Comparing Methods of Monitoring Home Detention: The Results of a Field Experiment," San Francisco: paper presented at the meeting of the American Society of Criminology, 1991.

Blumstein, Alfred, "The Context of Recent Changes in Crime Rates," in National Institute of Justice and the Executive Office for Weed and Seed, *What Can the Federal Government Do To Decrease Crime and Revitalize Communities?* Washington, DC, 1998, pp. 15–19.

Blumstein, Alfred, "Science and Technology Challenges Facing the Criminal Justice System in the United States," presentation at the Crime Technology Initiative Forum, Washington, DC, July 2000.

Board of Inquiry, "Rampart Area Corruption Incident: Executive Summary," Los Angeles: Los Angeles Police Department, 2000.

Boehlert, Sherwood, letter to Bruce Don, Director, Science and Technology Policy Institute at RAND, dated April 2, 2001.

Brin, David, *The Transparent Society*, Perseus Books (Addison-Wesley), 1998, http://crit.org/openness/sourcedocs/BrinCh1.html.

California State Auditor, Forensic Laboratories: Many Face Challenges Beyond Accreditation to Assure the Highest Quality Service, December, 1998, Available at http://www.bsa.ca.gov/bsa/pdfs/97025.pdf.

Caplan, Marc, private communication, 2001.

Centers for Disease Control and Prevention, "The Violence-Related Attitudes and Behaviors of High School Students—New York City, 1992," *Morbidity and Mortality Weekly Report*, 42:773–777, 1993.

Computer Security Institute, "Issues and Trends: 1999 CSI/FBI Computer Crime and Security Survey," announced March 1999, cited in the U.S. General Accounting Office, *Critical Infrastructure Protection: Comprehensive Strategy Can Draw on Year 2000 Experiences*, Washington, DC: U.S. General Accounting Office, October 1999.

Connors, Edward, et al., *Convicted by Juries, Exonerated by Science: Case Studies in the Use of DNA Evidence to Establish Innocence After Trial*, Washington, DC: U.S. Department of Justice, National Institute of Justice, NCJ 177626, September 1999.

Crime Prevention Panel, *Just Around the Corner*, London: Foresight, March 2000.

Davis, Lois M., William Schwabe, and Ronald Fricker, *Challenges and Choices for Crime-Fighting Technology: Results from Two Nationwide Surveys*, Santa Monica, Calif.: RAND, 2001.

Dertouzos, Michael, *What Will Be: How the New World of Information Will Change Our Lives*, San Francisco: HarperSanFrancisco, 1997.

Dwyer, K., D. Osher, and C. Warger, *Early Warning, Timely Response: A Guide to Safe Schools,* Washington, DC: U.S. Department of Education, 1998. The full text of this public domain publication is available at the Department's home page at http://www.ed.gov/offices/OSERS/OSEP/earlywrn.html.

FBI, "Terrorism in the United States: 1995," Washington, DC: U.S. Department of Justice, Federal Bureau of Investigation, National Security Division, Terrorist Research and Analytical Center, http://www.securitymanagement.com/fbir.html, 1995.

Gaudiani, Claire L., "Wisdom as Capital in Prosperous Communities," in Frances Hesselbein et al. (eds.), *The Community of the Future,* San Francisco: Jossey-Bass Publishers, 1998, pp. 59–69.

Goldberg, Andrew L., and Brian A. Reaves, *Sheriffs' Departments 1997,* Washington, DC: U.S. Department of Justice, Office of Justice Programs, Bureau of Justice Statistics, February 2000.

Gottlieb, Steven, Sheldon Arenberg, and Raj Singh, *Crime Analysis: From First Report to Final Arrest,* Montclair, Calif.: Alpha Publishing, 1994.

Governor's Office of Emergency Services (OES), *Local Planning Guidance on Terrorism Response,* Sacramento, Calif.: OES, 1998.

Green, Mary W., *The Appropriate and Effective Use of Security Technologies in U.S. Schools: A Guide for Schools and Law Enforcement Agencies.* Washington, DC: U.S. Department of Justice, National Institute of Justice, September 1999.

Human Rights Watch, "Shielded from Justice: Police Brutality and Accountability in the United States," http://www.hrw.org/reports98/police, 1998.

Huxley, Aldous, *Brave New World,* New York: Harper's, 1932.

Imel, Kathy J., and James W. Hart, *Understanding Wireless Communications in Public Safety: A Guidebook to Technology, Issues, Planning, and Management,* National Law Enforcement and Corrections Technology Center, Rocky Mountain Region, March 2000.

Institute for Law and Justice, "Crime Policy for the 21st Century: A Brainstorming Session (Summary Report)," Washington, DC: National Institute of Justice and Office of Policy Development, U.S. Department of Justice, June 8, 1999.

Institute for Law and Justice, *Future Plan: Taking Community Policing to the Next Level*, Alexandria, Va., 1999.

Law Enforcement and Corrections Technology Advisory Council (LECTAC), "Annual Meeting Report (Draft)," Charleston, SC: National Law Enforcement and Corrections Technology Center, March 10, 2000, cited as "LECTAC, 2000."

Lawrence, James H., presentation at the Conference on Technologies for Public Safety in Critical Incident Response, Denver, June 10, 2000.

Lindesmith Center, "The Lindesmith Center Calls for Just New York Policing, an End to Operation Condor," (http://www.lindesmith.org/news/DailyNews/ 03_22_2000condor.html), March 22, 2000.

Little, R. J. A., and D. B. Rubin, *Statistical Analysis with Missing Data*, John Wiley & Sons, New York, N.Y., 1987.

Lothridge, Kevin, informal communication, 2000.

Mamalian, Cynthia, and Nancy G. LaVigne, *The Use of Computerized Crime Mapping by Law Enforcement: Survey Results*, Washington, DC: National Institute of Justice, January 1999.

Mitchell, Andy, Statement on Domestic Preparedness Efforts before the Subcommittee on Youth Violence and the Subcommittee on Technology, Terrorism and Government Information, Committee on the Judiciary, U.S. Senate, April 20, 1999.

Moore, Duncan T., letter dated August 18, 2000.

Morgan, M. Granger, "Risk Analysis and Management," *Scientific American*, July 1993, p. 33.

Meyer, Greg, "Nonlethal Weapons versus Conventional Police Tactics: The Los Angeles Police Department Experience," Los Angeles: California State University (master's thesis), 1991.

Meyer, Greg, "Nonlethal Weapons versus Conventional Police Tactics: Assessing Injuries and Liabilities," *The Police Chief*, August 1992, pp. 10–15.

National Commission on the Future of DNA Evidence, *Postconviction DNA Testing: Recommendations for Handling Requests*, Washington, DC: U.S. Department of Justice, National Institute of Justice, NCJ 161258, June 1996, cited as "DNA Commission, 1999."

National Partnership for Reinventing Government (NPR), *Mapping Out Crime: Providing 21st Century Tools for Safe Communities*, http://www.npr.gov/library/papers/bkgrd/crimemap.

NCES/BJS, *Indicators of School Crime and Safety, 2000*, Washington, DC: U.S. Department of Education, Office of Educational Research and Improvement, National Center for Education Statistics and U.S. Department of Justice, Office of Justice Programs, Bureau of Justice Statistics, 2000.

Newton, Jim, and Tina Daunt, "City Reaches Deal with U.S. on Police Reform Package," *Los Angeles Times*, November 1, 2000, p. B7.

Nichiporuk, Brian, and Carl H. Builder, *Information Technologies and the Future of Land Warfare*, Santa Monica, Calif.: RAND, 1995.

Norris, Clive, and Gary Armstrong, *The Maximum Surveillance Society: The Rise of CCTV*, Oxford: Berg, 1999.

O'Connell, John P., "Community Crime Analysis," in National Institute of Justice and the Executive Office for Weed and Seed, *What Can the Federal Government Do To Decrease Crime and Revitalize Communities?* Washington, DC, 1998, pp. 87–95.

OES, State of California Emergency Plan, Sacramento, Calif.: Governor's Office of Emergency Services, 1998.

OJJDP, *Promising Strategies To Reduce Gun Violence*, Washington, DC: U.S. Department of Justice, Office of Justice Programs, Office of Juvenile Justice and Delinquency Prevention, 1999.

Opinion Research Corporation International, *Privacy, Technology and Criminal Justice Information: Public Attitudes toward Uses of*

Criminal History Information, Washington, DC: Bureau of Justice Statistics, 2000.

Orwell, George, *1984,* New York: Harcourt, Brace, 1949.

Parks, Bernard C., Chief of Police, Los Angeles Police Department, *Board of Inquiry into the Rampart Area Corruption Incident,* March 1, 2000.

President's Commission, *Critical Foundations: Protecting America's Infrastructures,* Washington, DC: President's Commission on Critical Infrastructure Protection, 1997.

Reaves, Brian A., and Andrew L. Goldberg, *Law Enforcement Management and Administrative Statistics, 1997: Data for Individual State and Local Agencies with 100 or More Officers,* Washington, DC: U.S. Department of Justice, Office of Justice Programs, Bureau of Justice Statistics, April 1999.

Reaves, Brian A., and Andrew L. Goldberg, *Local Police Departments 1997,* Washington, DC: U.S. Department of Justice, Office of Justice Programs, Bureau of Justice Statistics, February 2000.

Rich, Thomas F., *The Use of Computerized Mapping in Crime Control and Prevention Programs,* Washington, DC: National Institute of Justice, 1995.

Sandia National Laboratories, *Strategies for Preserving Our National Security: US Infrastructure Assurance Strategic Roadmaps,* 1998.

Scheck, Barry, Peter Neufeld, and Jim Dwyer, *Actual Innocence,* New York: Doubleday, 2000.

Schwabe, William, *Needs and Prospects for Crime-Fighting Technology: The Federal Role in Assisting State and Local Law Enforcement,* Santa Monica, Calif.: RAND, 1999.

Shah, B. V., Barnwell, B. G., and G. S. Bieler, *SUDAAN User's Manual,* Release 7.5, Research Triangle Park: Research Triangle Institute, 1997.

Sheppo, Michael G., Testimony before the U.S. House of Representatives Committee on the Judiciary Subcommittee on Crime, March 23, 2000.

Sherman, Lawrence W., et al., *Preventing Crime: What Works, What Doesn't, What's Promising,* College Park, Md.: University of Maryland, Department of Criminology and Criminal Justice, 1997.

Skinner, C. J., D. Holt, and T. M. F. Smith, eds., *Analysis of Complex Surveys,* John Wiley & Sons, New York, 1989.

States' Coalition, "Crime Laboratory Crisis Information Package," 1999. For more information, contact Gale Buckner, Director of Legislative and Inter-Governmental Affairs, Georgia Bureau of Investigation, at (404) 244-2501.

Steadman, Greg W., *Survey of DNA Crime Laboratories, 1998,* Washington, DC: Bureau of Justice Statistics, 2000.

Steinhardt, Barry, "ACLU Calls on Law Enforcement to Support Privacy Laws for Public Video Surveillance," Washington, DC: American Civil Liberties Union, press release, April 8, 1999.

Stephan, James J., *State Prison Expenditures, 1996,* Washington, DC: Bureau of Justice Statistics, 1999.

Sterling, Claire, *Thieves' World: The Threat of the New Global Network of Organized Crime,* New York: Simon and Schuster, 1994.

Taylor, Mary J., Robert C. Epper, and Thomas K. Tolman, *State and Local Law Enforcement Wireless Communications and Interoperability: A Quantitative Analysis,* National Law Enforcement and Corrections Technology Center, Rocky Mountain Region, January 1998.

USA Today, Special Report, August 20–21, 1996.

Wilms, Wellford W., Warren H. Schmidt, and Alex J. Norman, *The Strain of Change: Voices of Los Angeles Police Officers,* Los Angeles: University of California, 2000.

Wilson, James Q., and George Kelling, "Broken Windows: The Police and Neighborhood Safety," *Atlantic Monthly,* March 1982. Reprinted in Wilson, James Q., *On Character,* Washington, DC: The AEI Press, 1995.